Imagination

Arya Bàhram

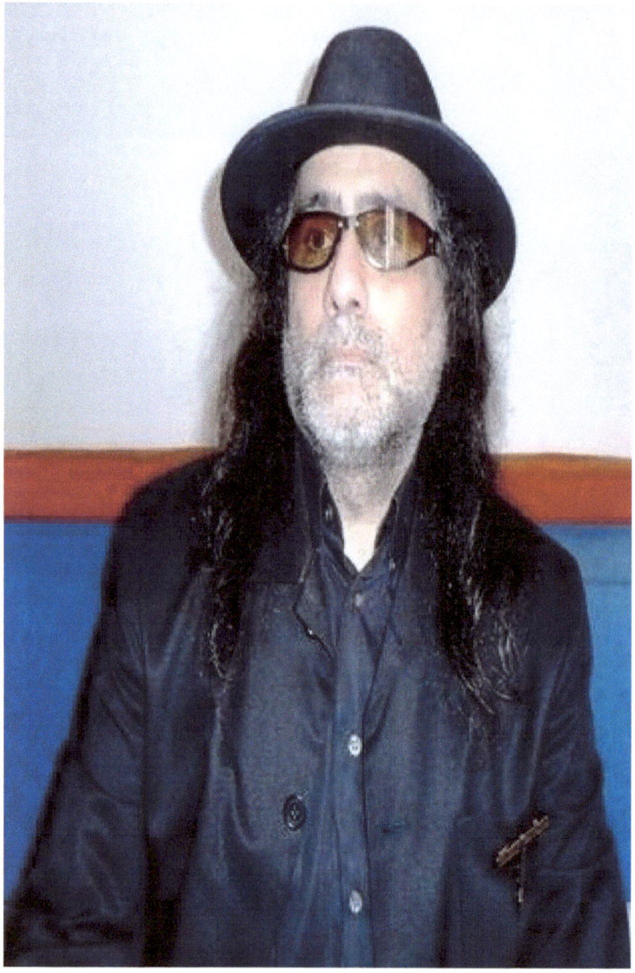

Imagination

Arya Bàhram

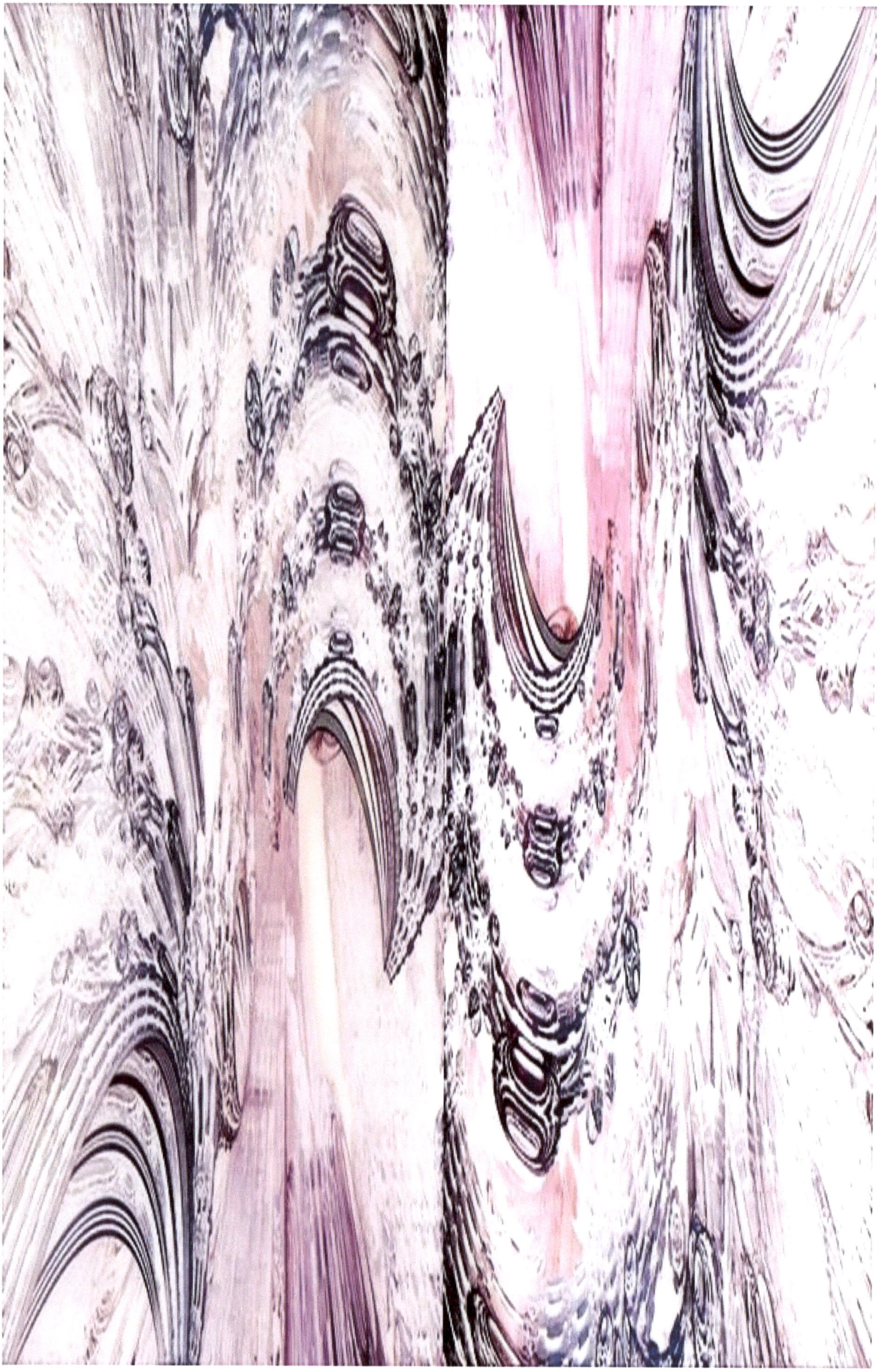

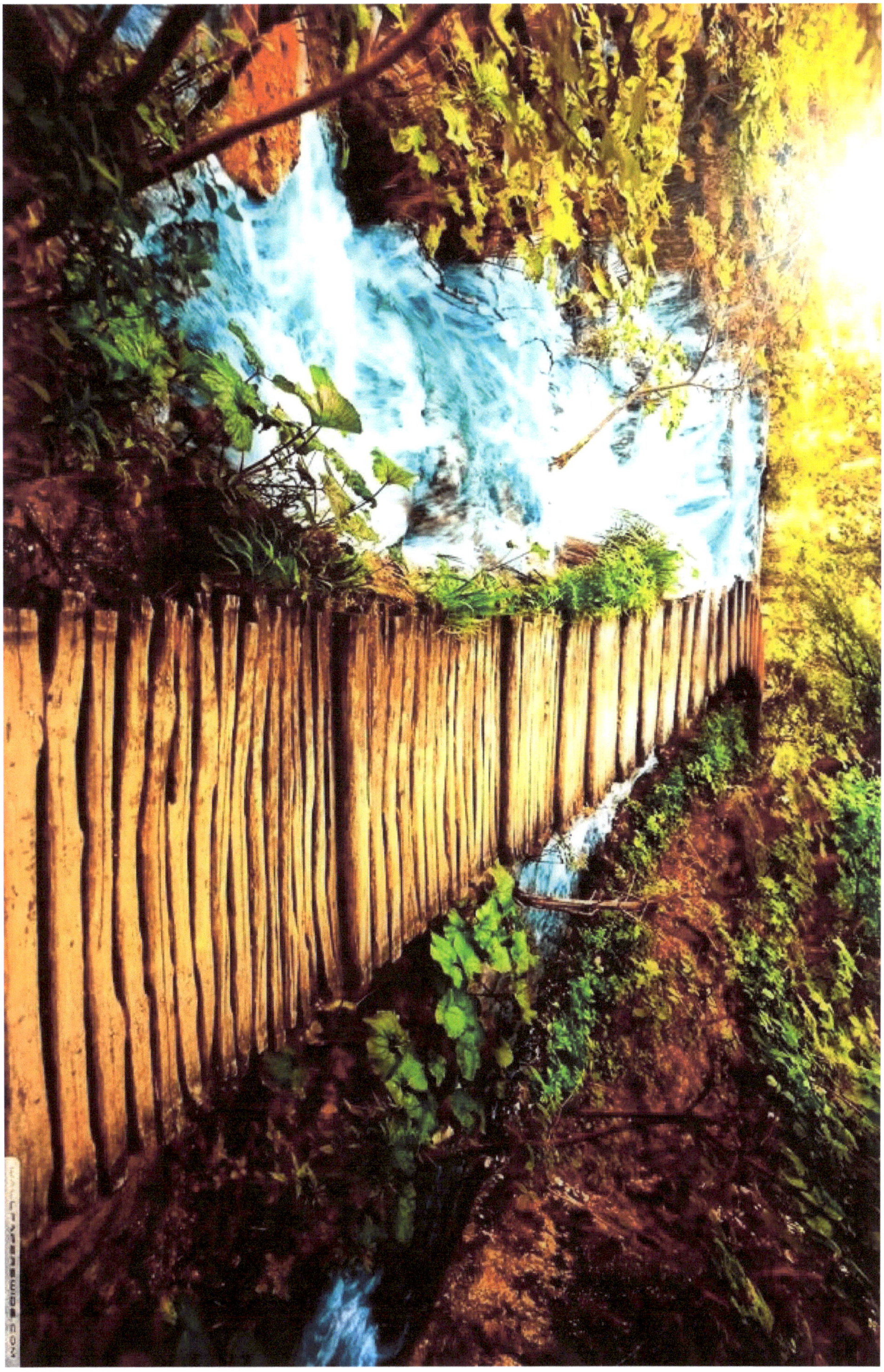

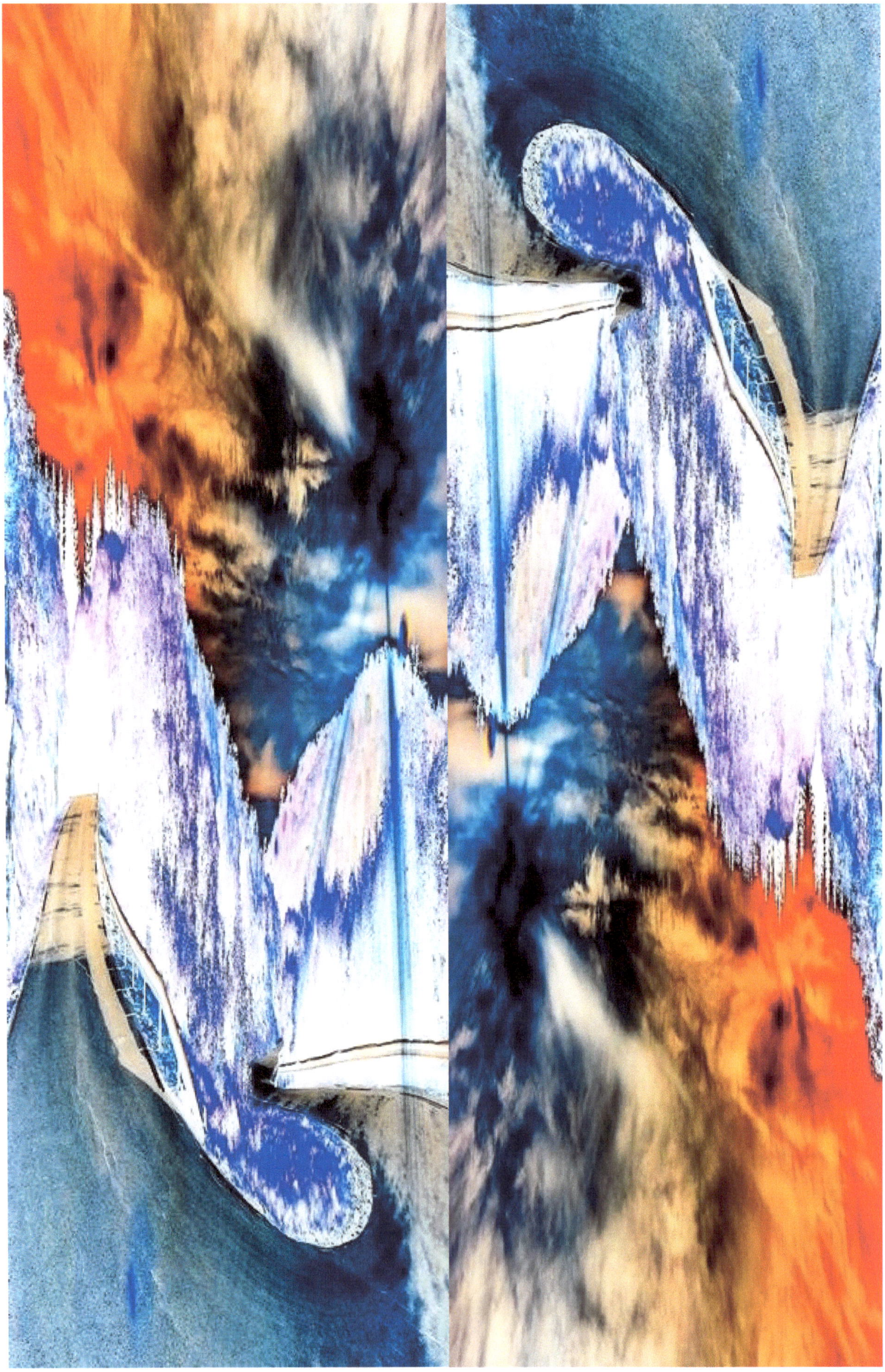

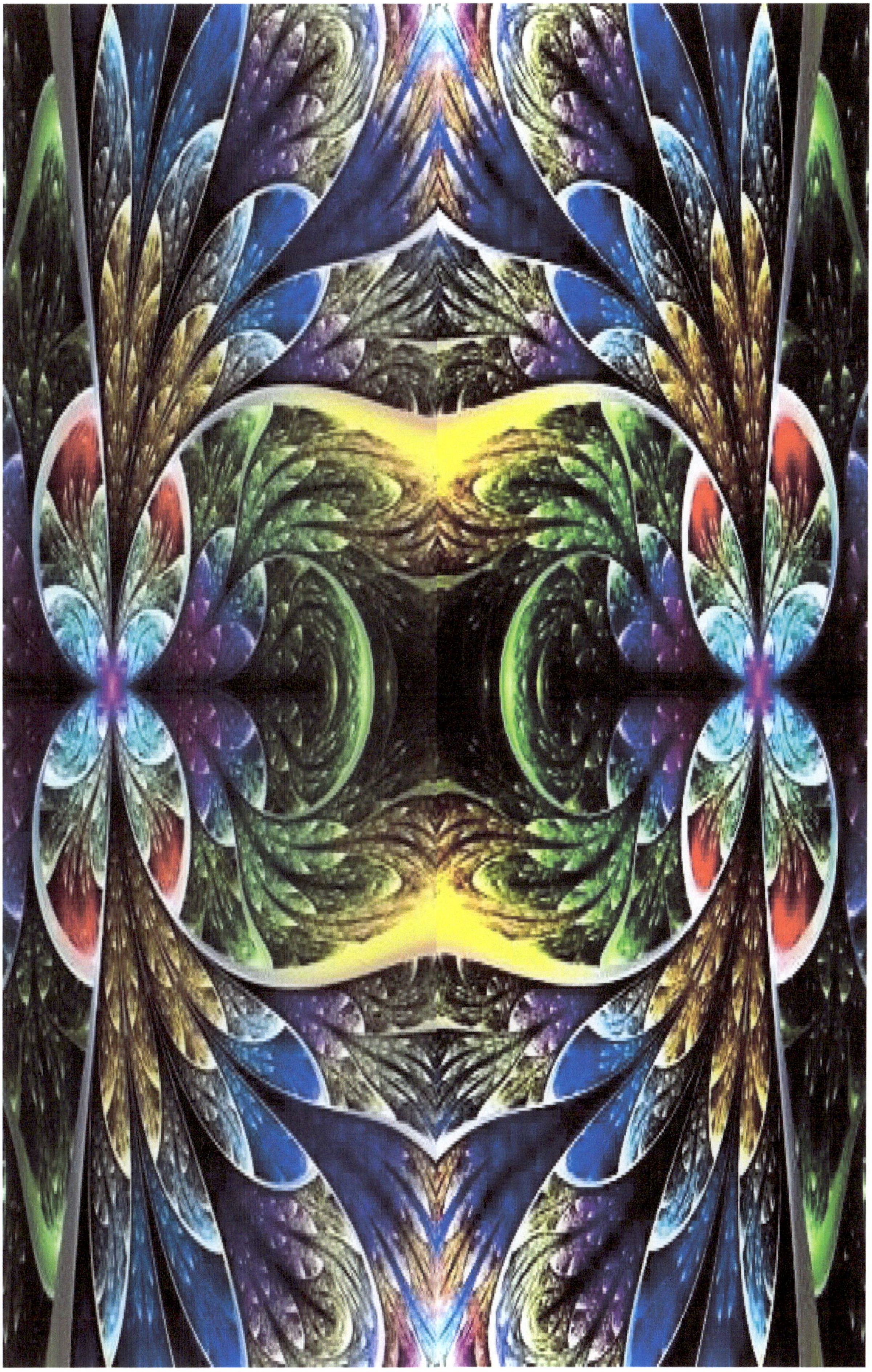

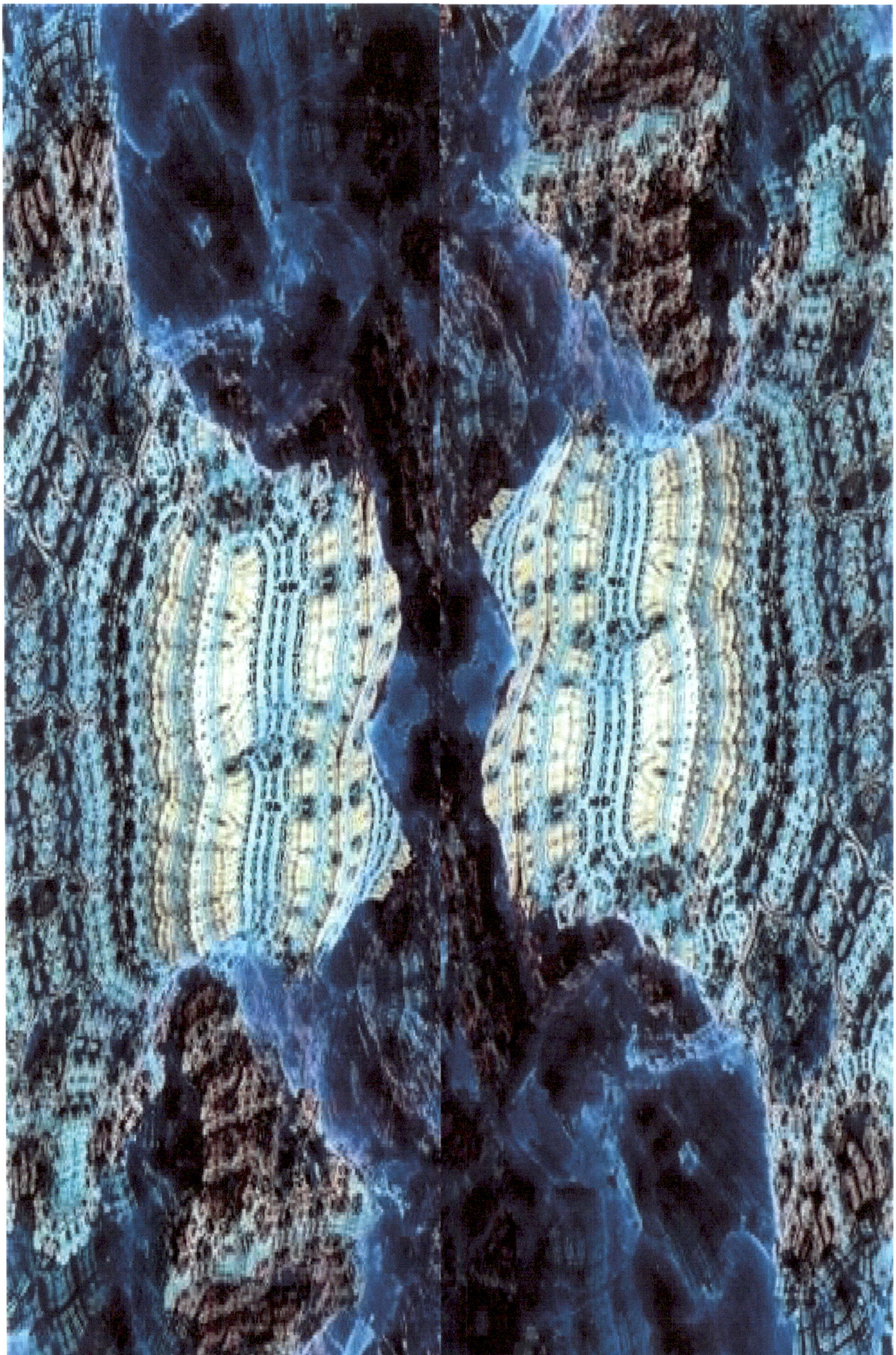

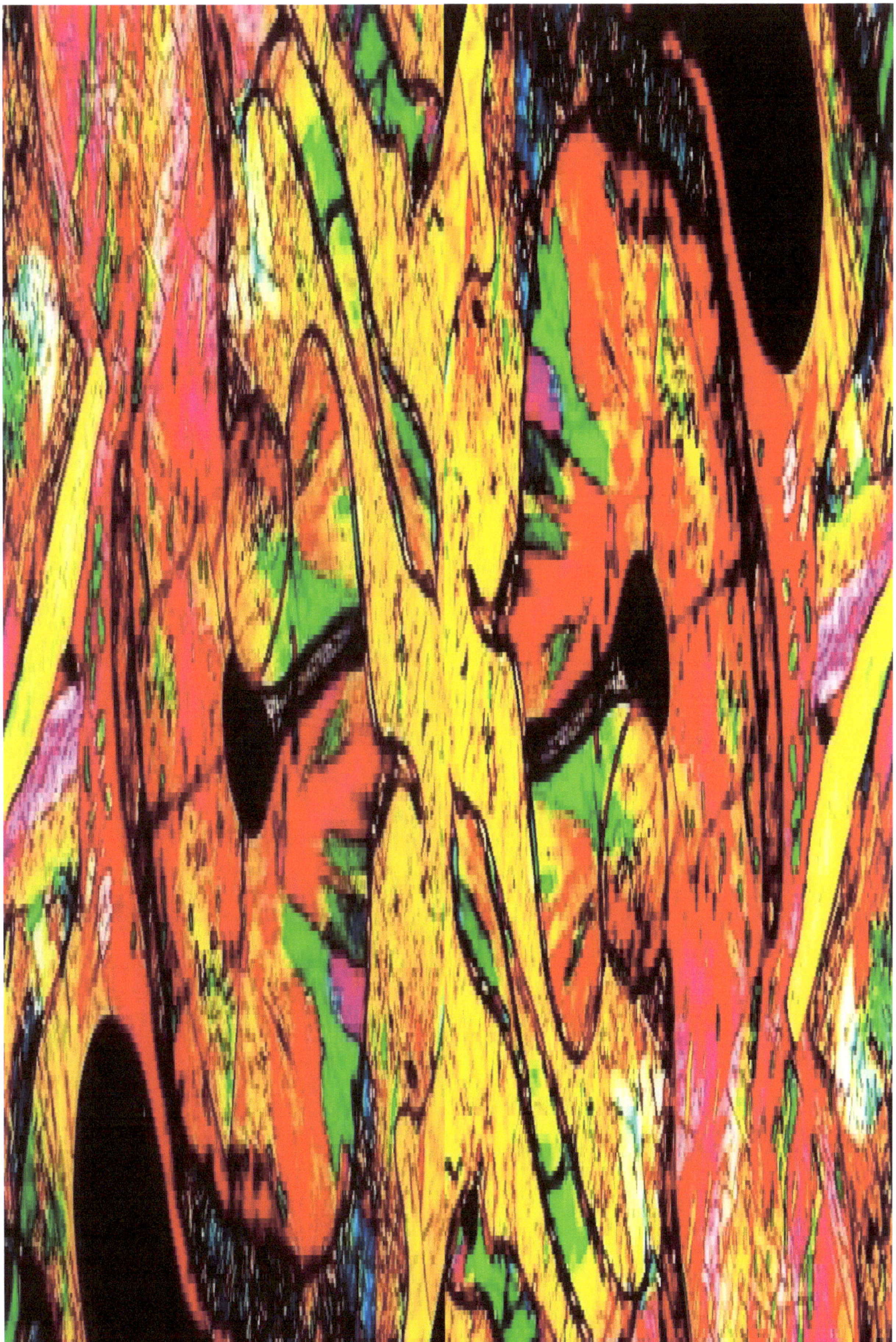

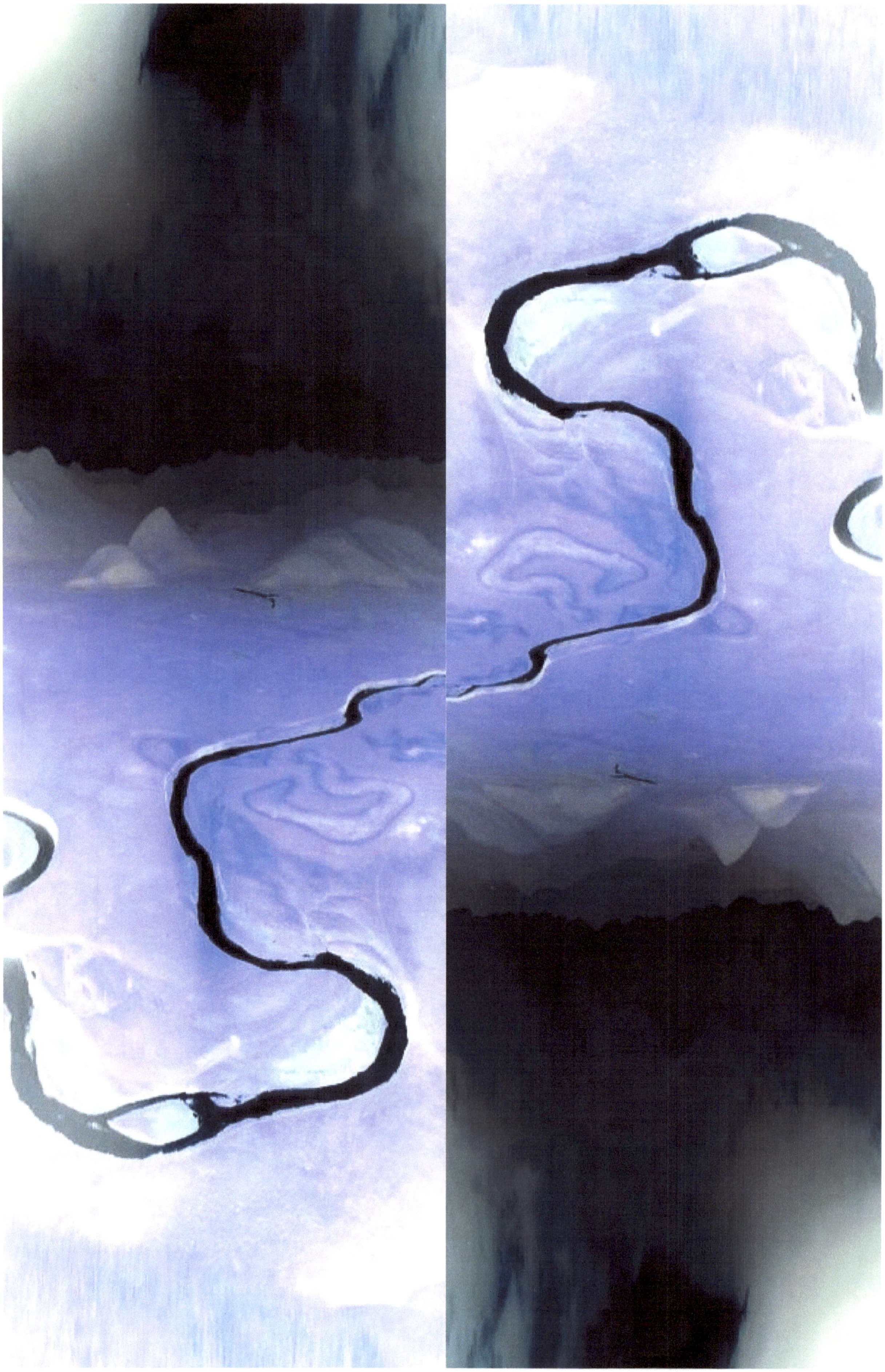

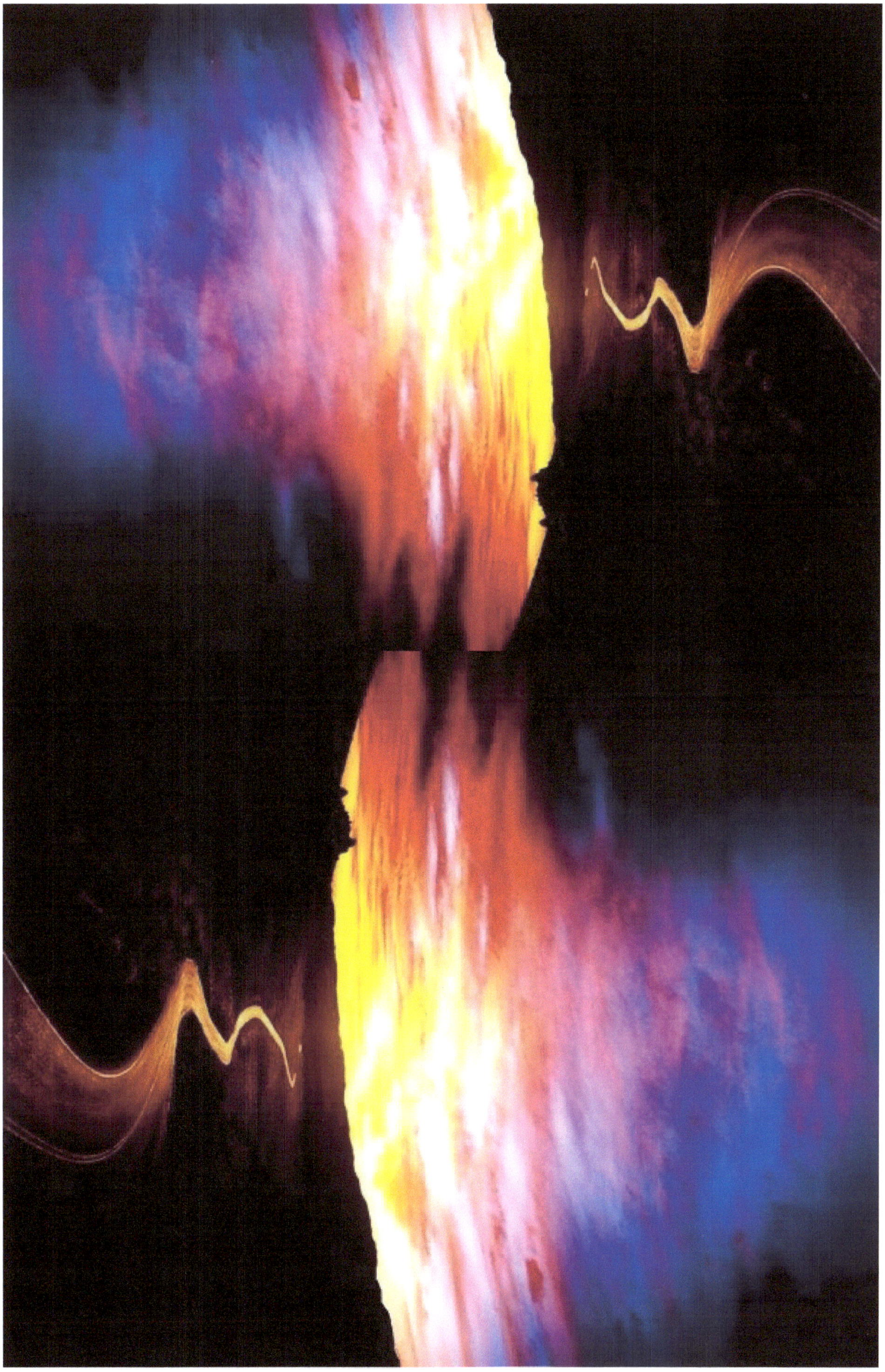

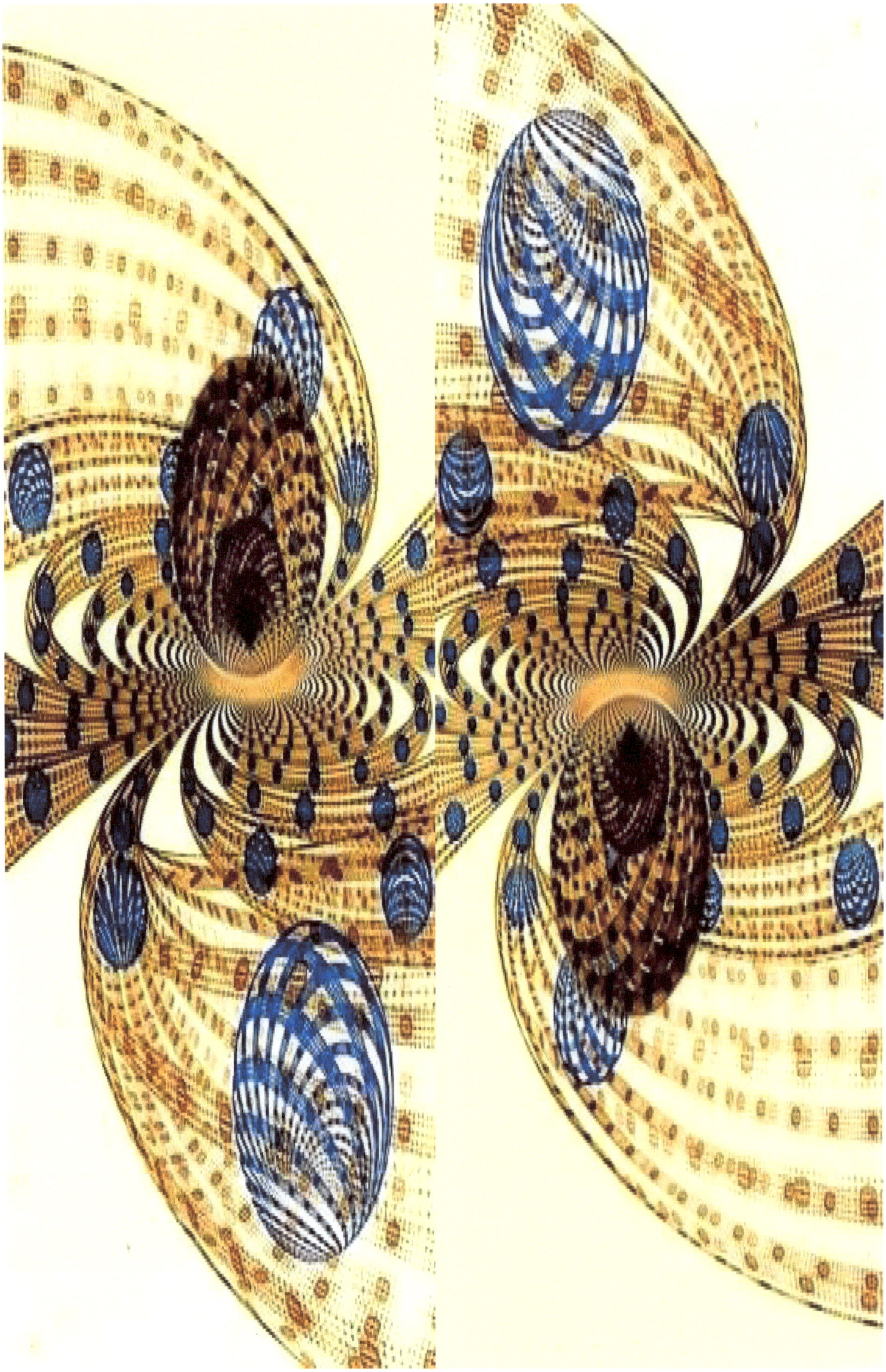

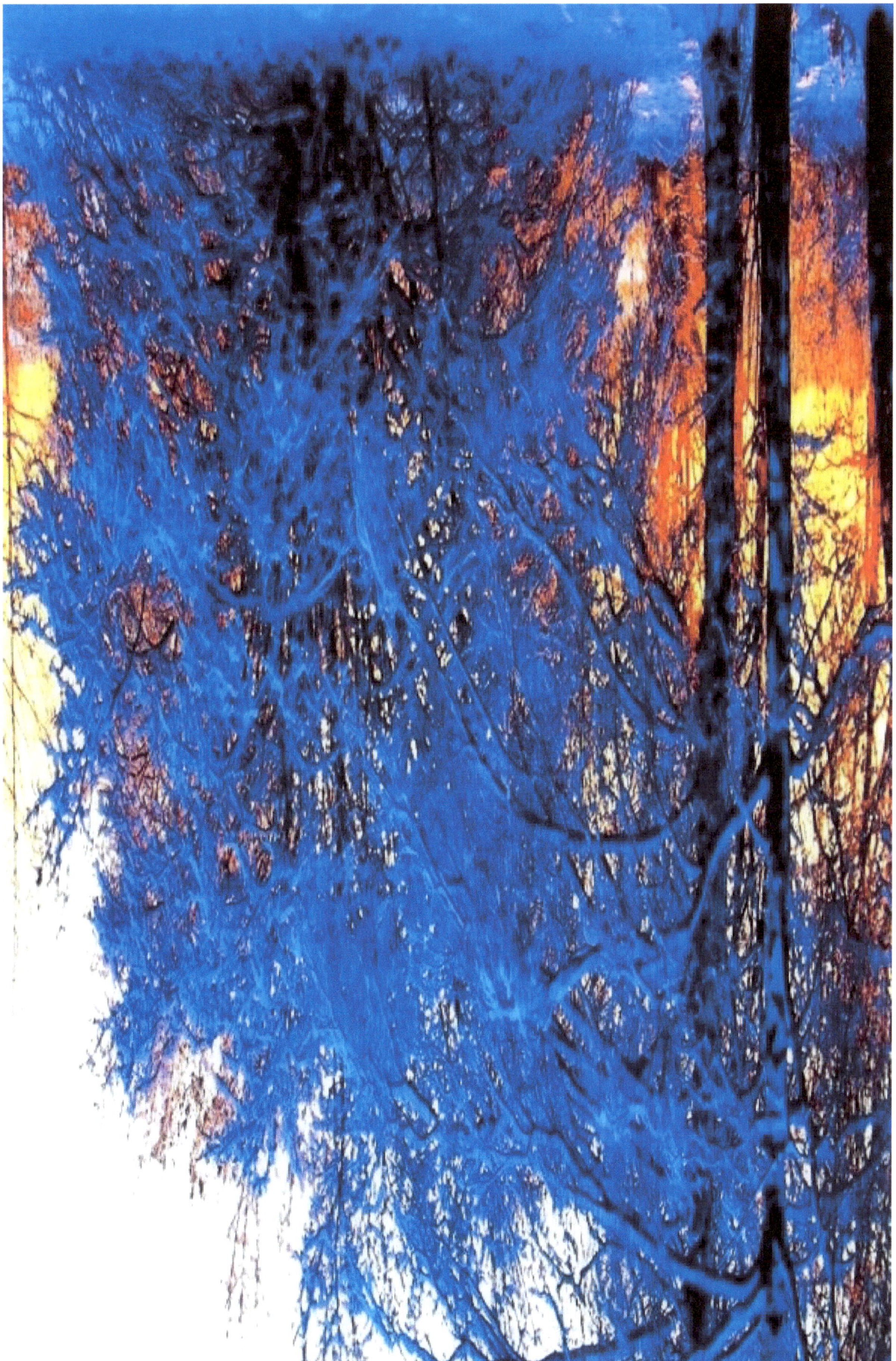

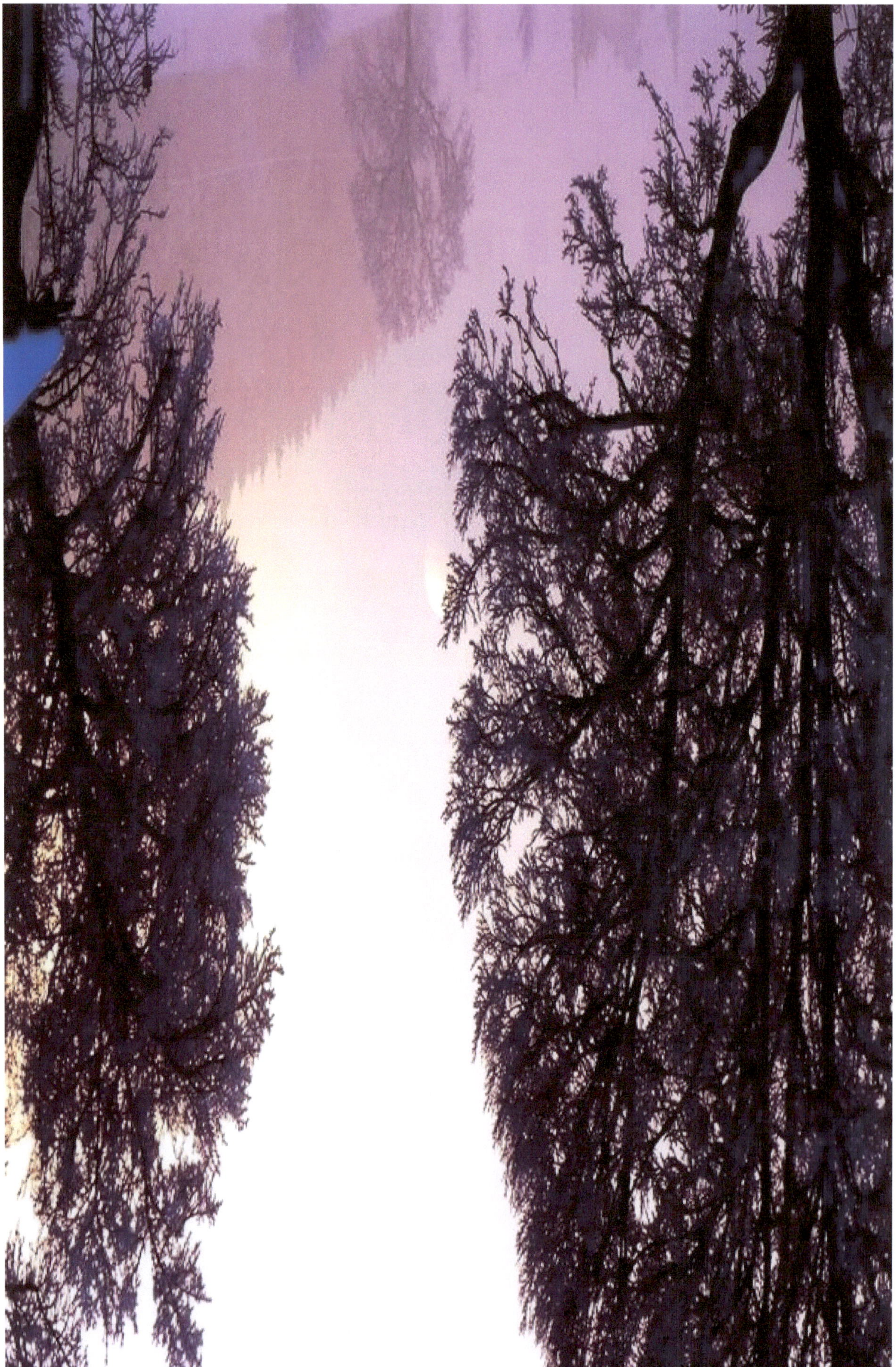

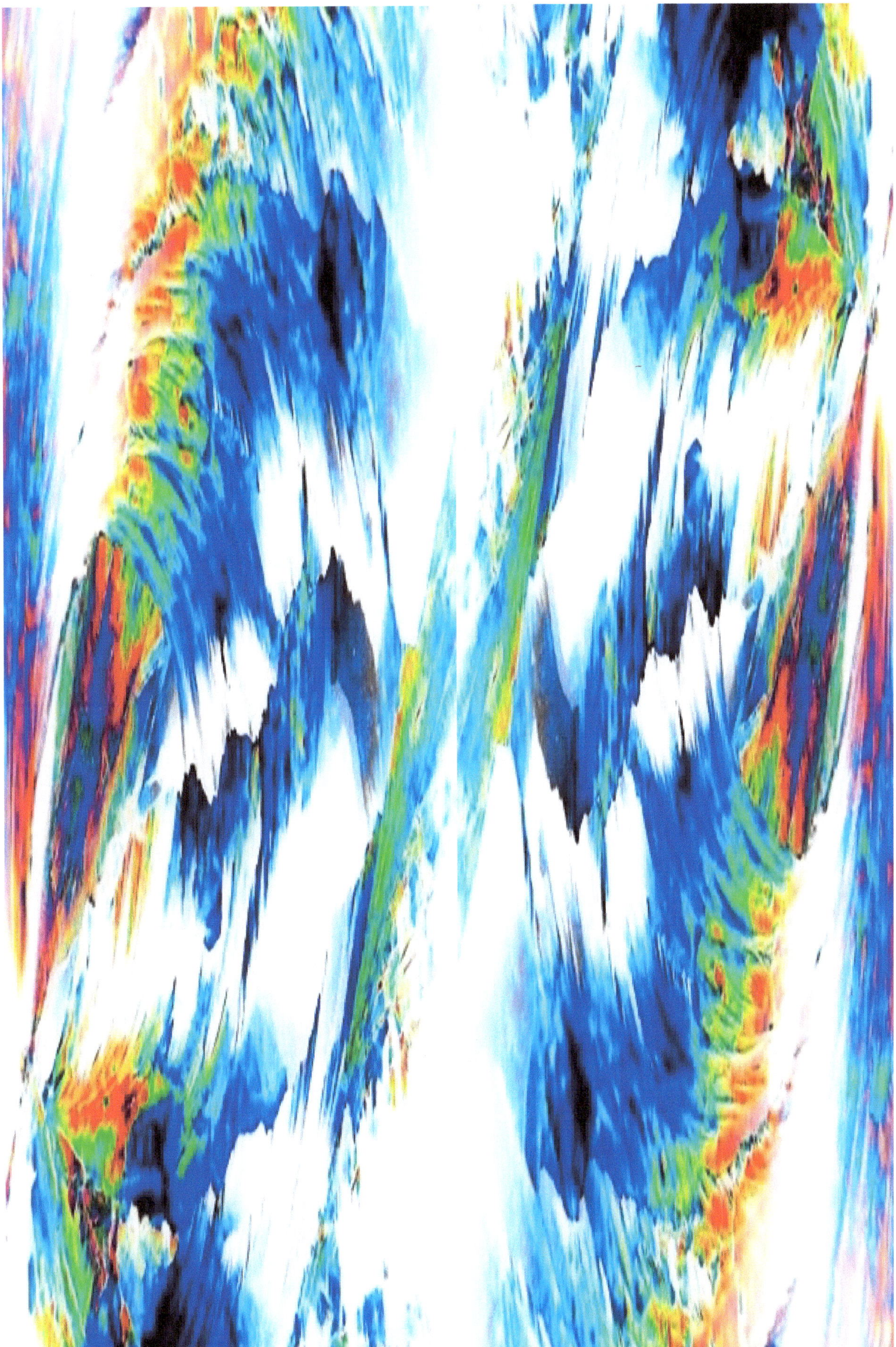

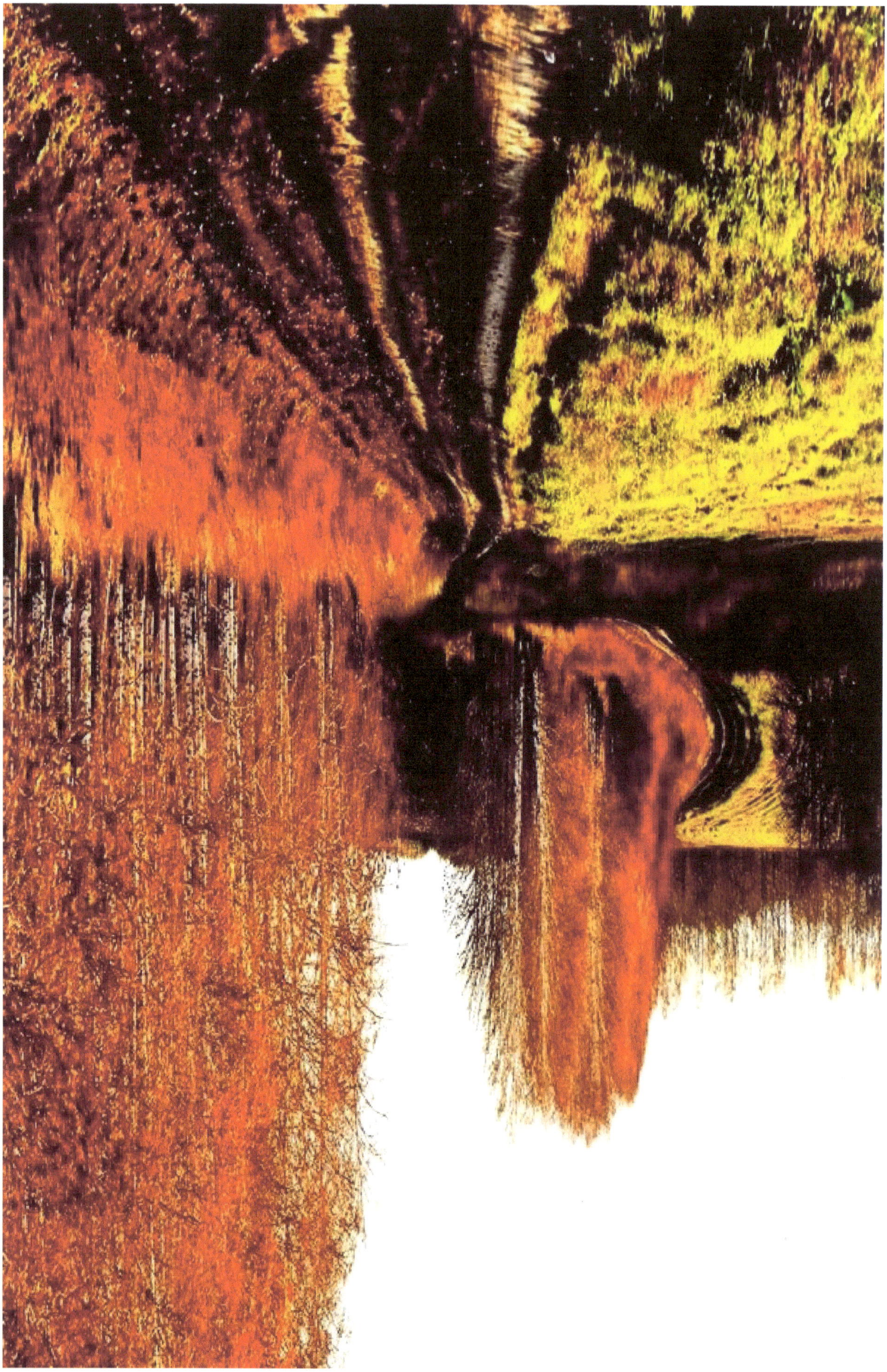

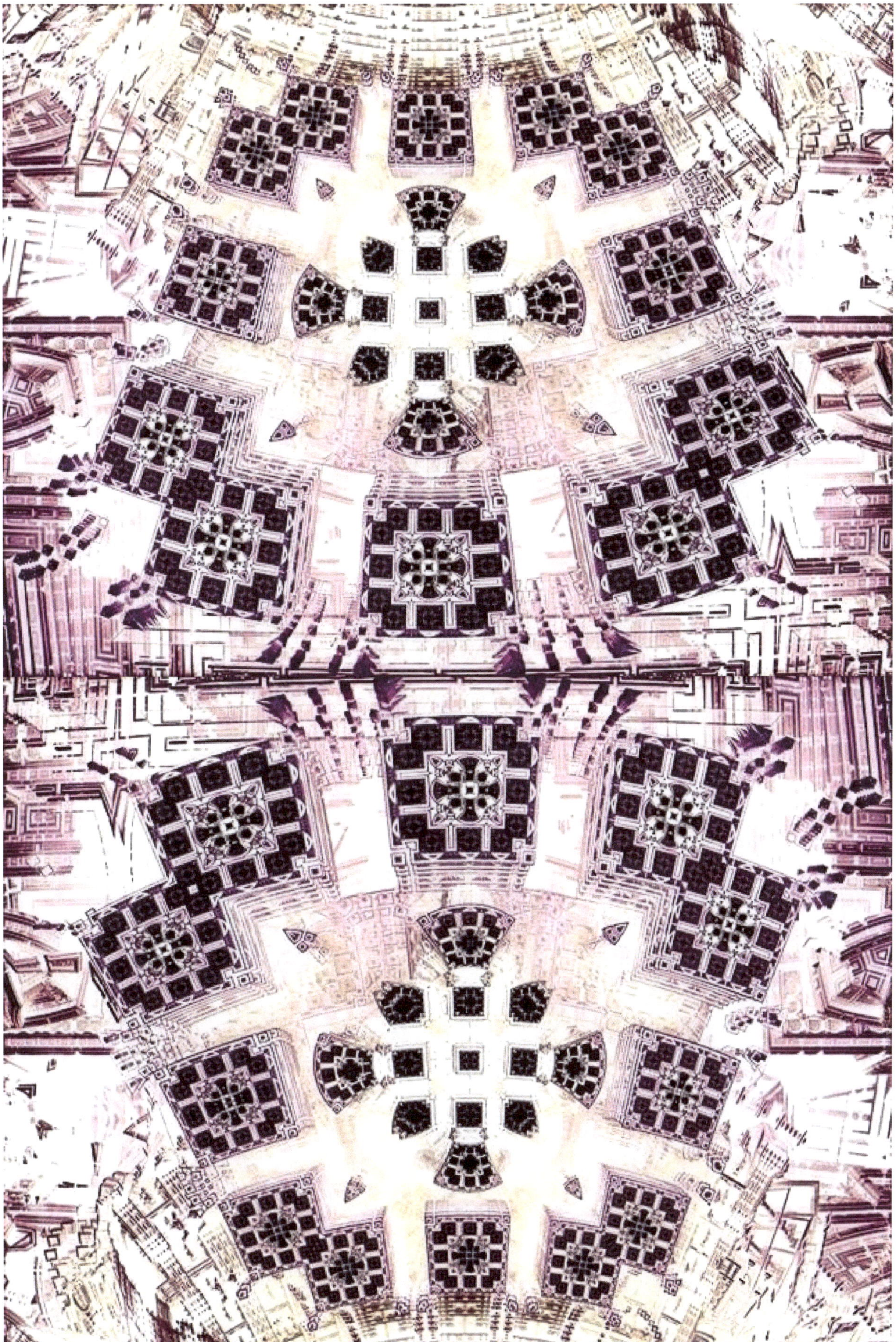

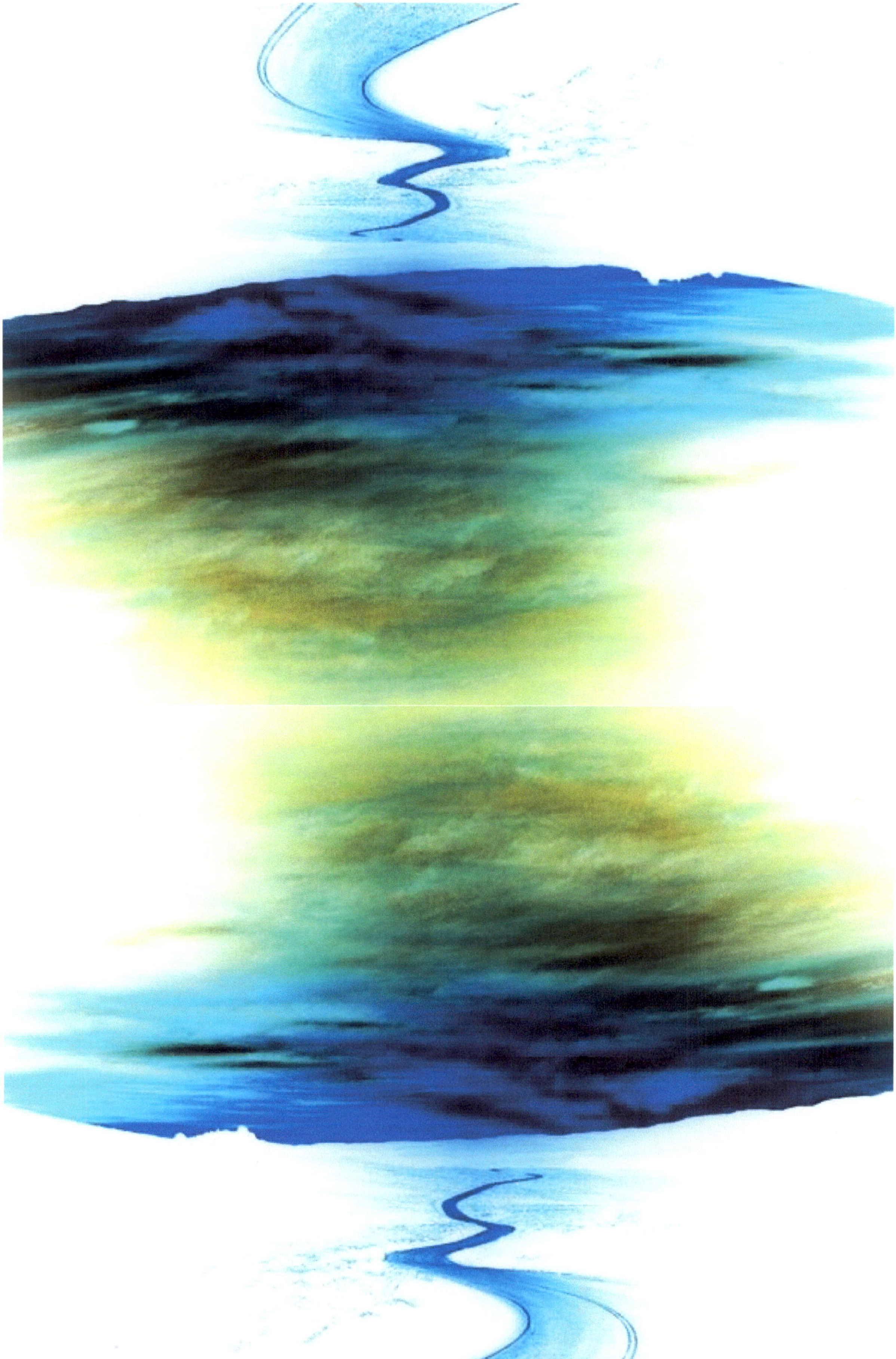

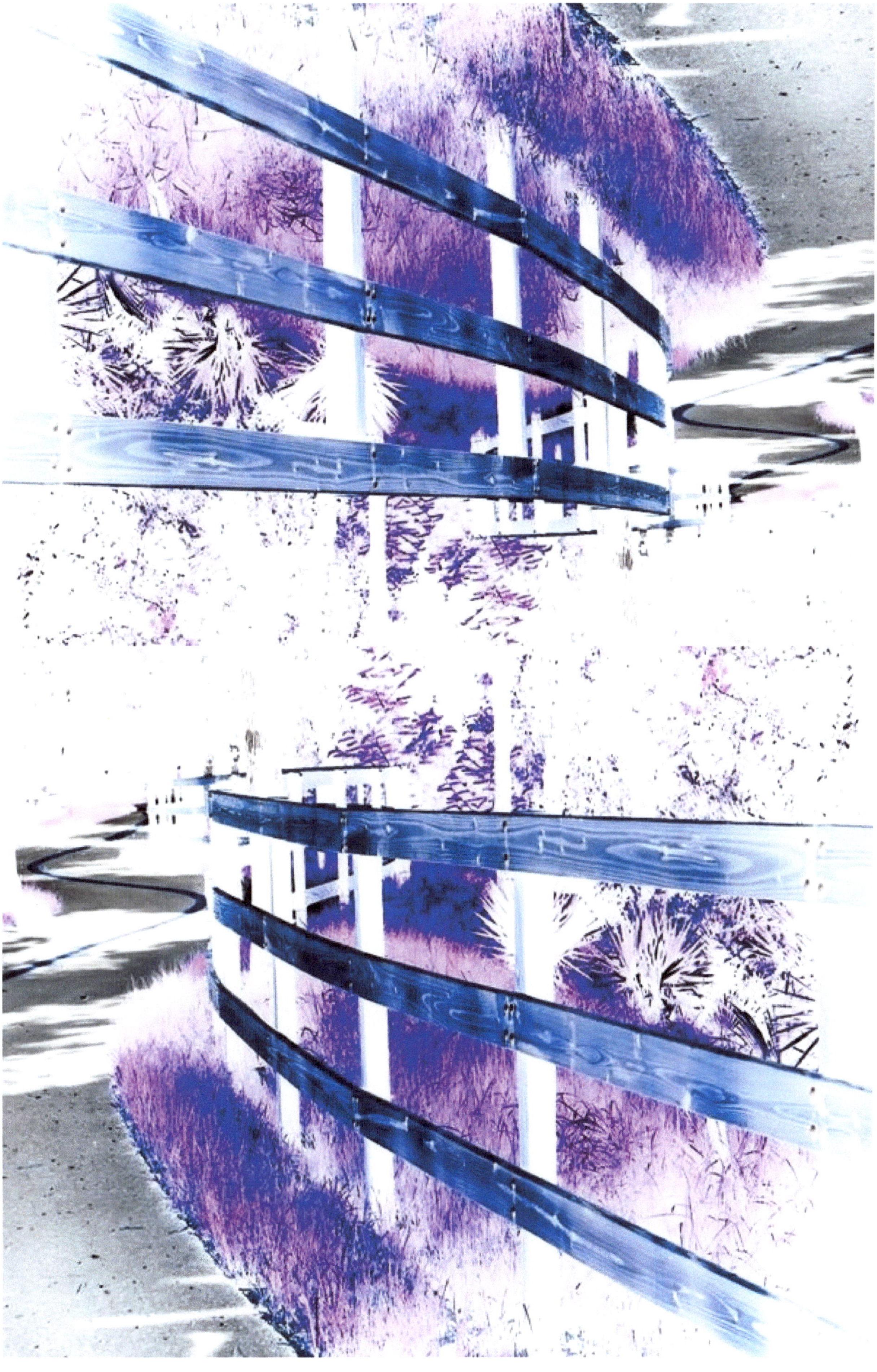

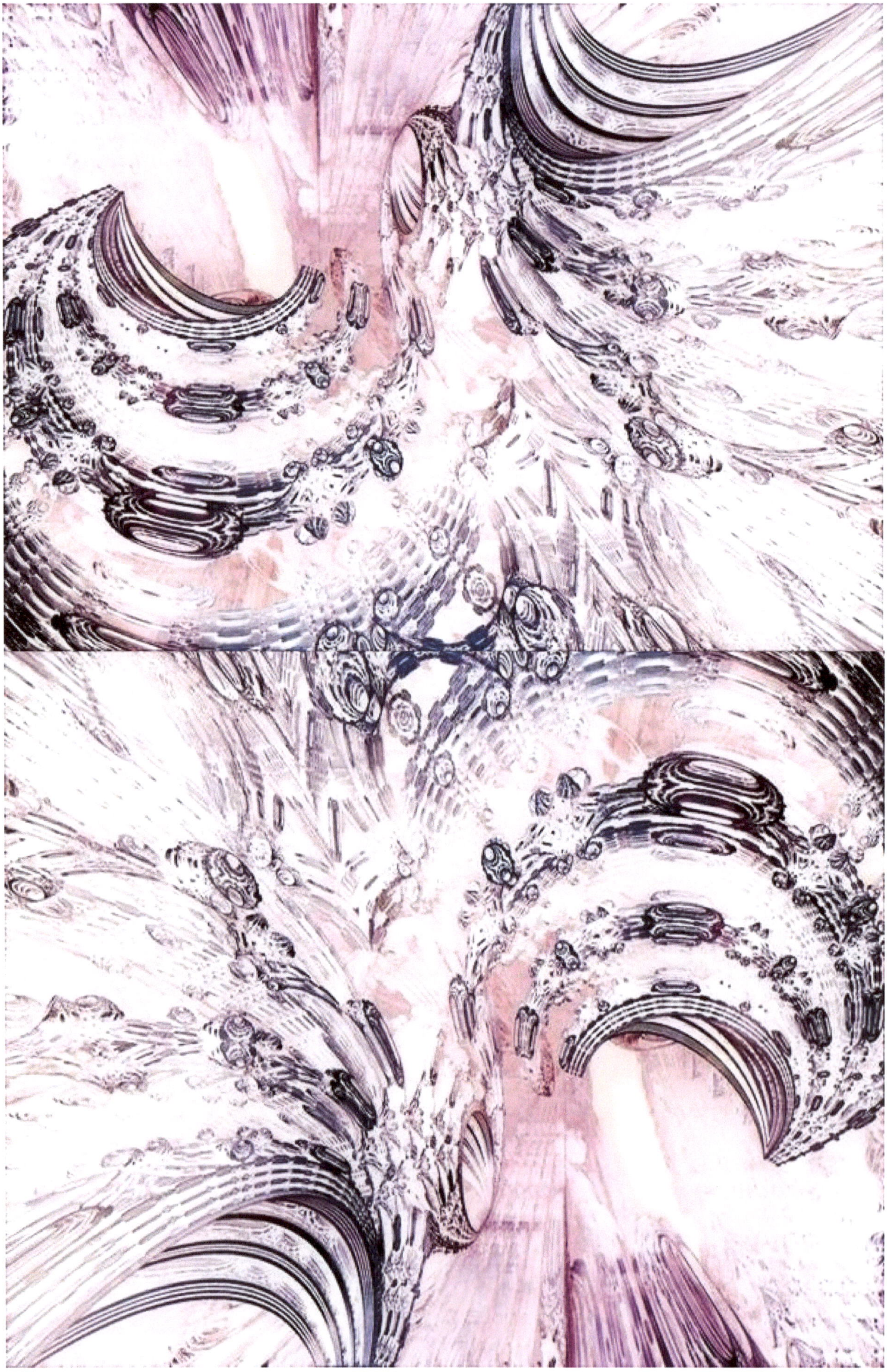

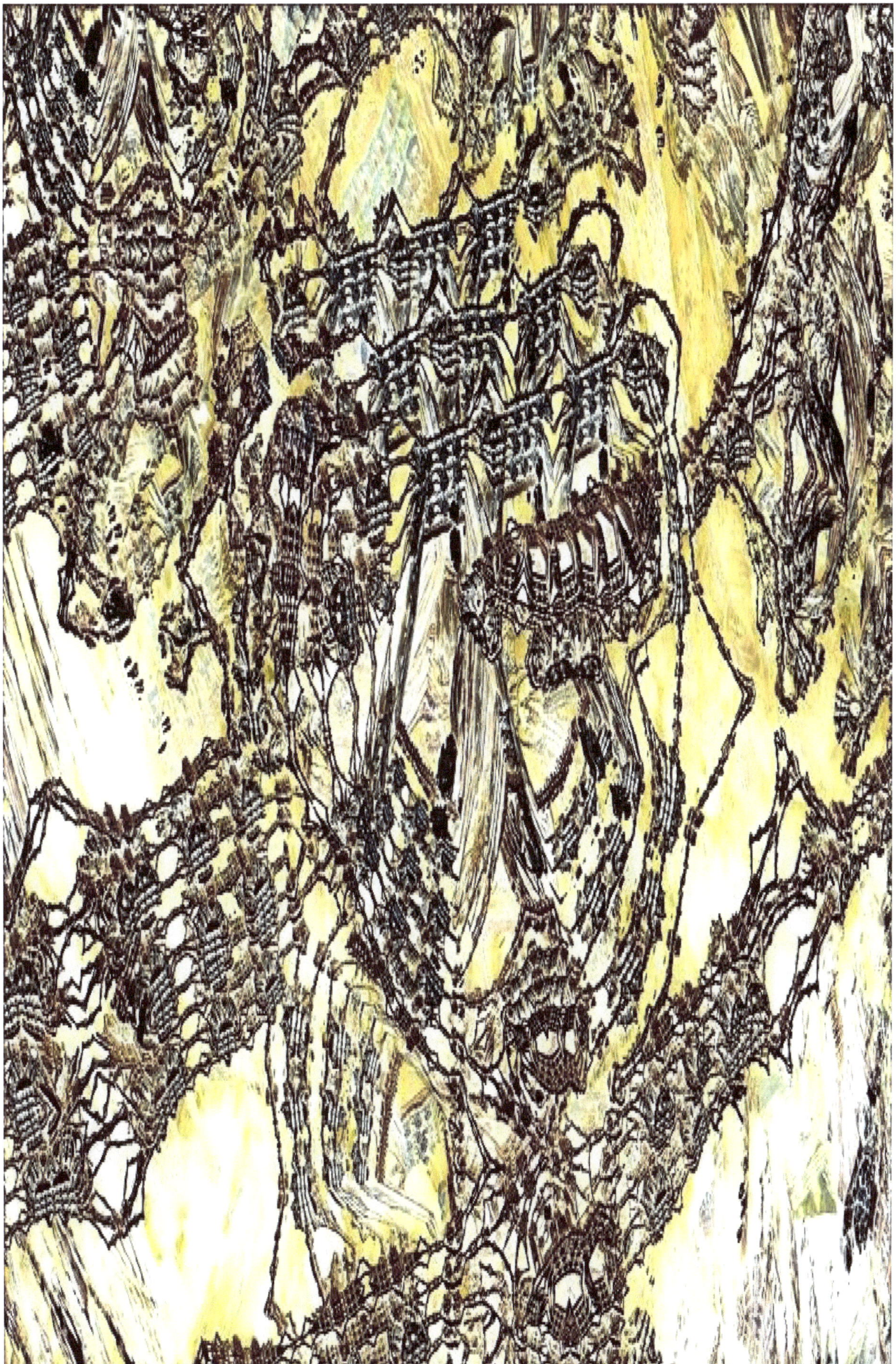

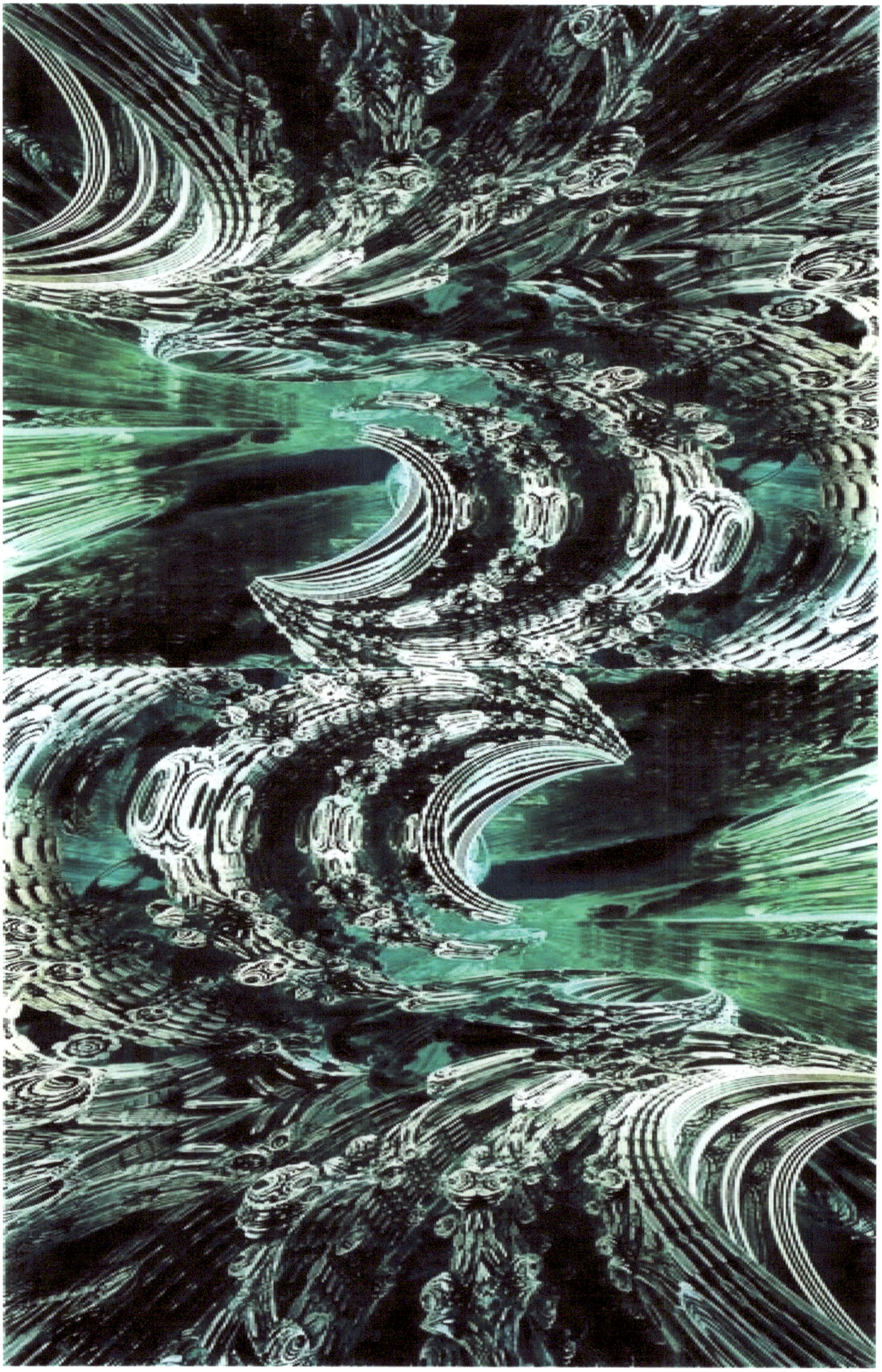

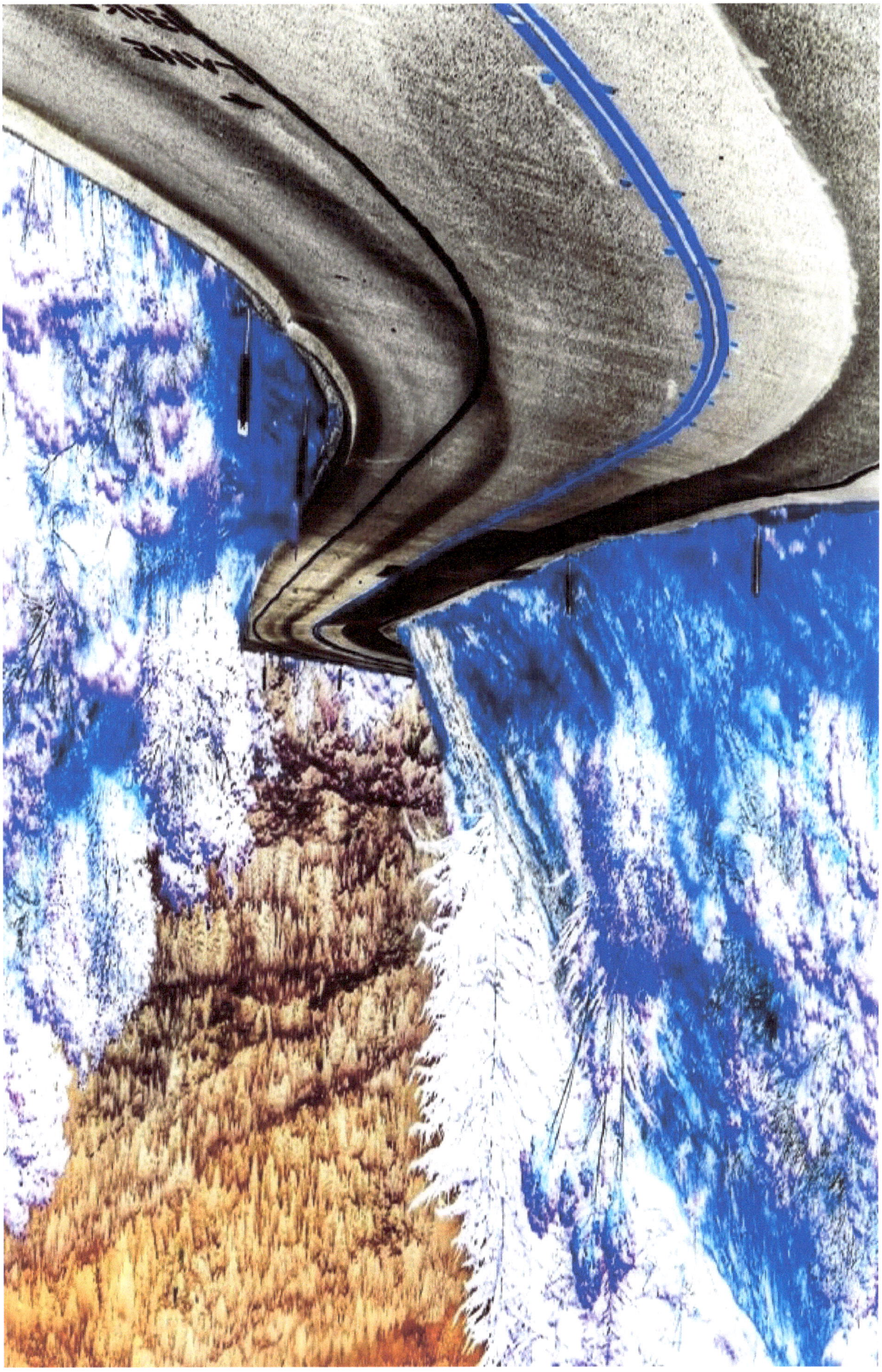

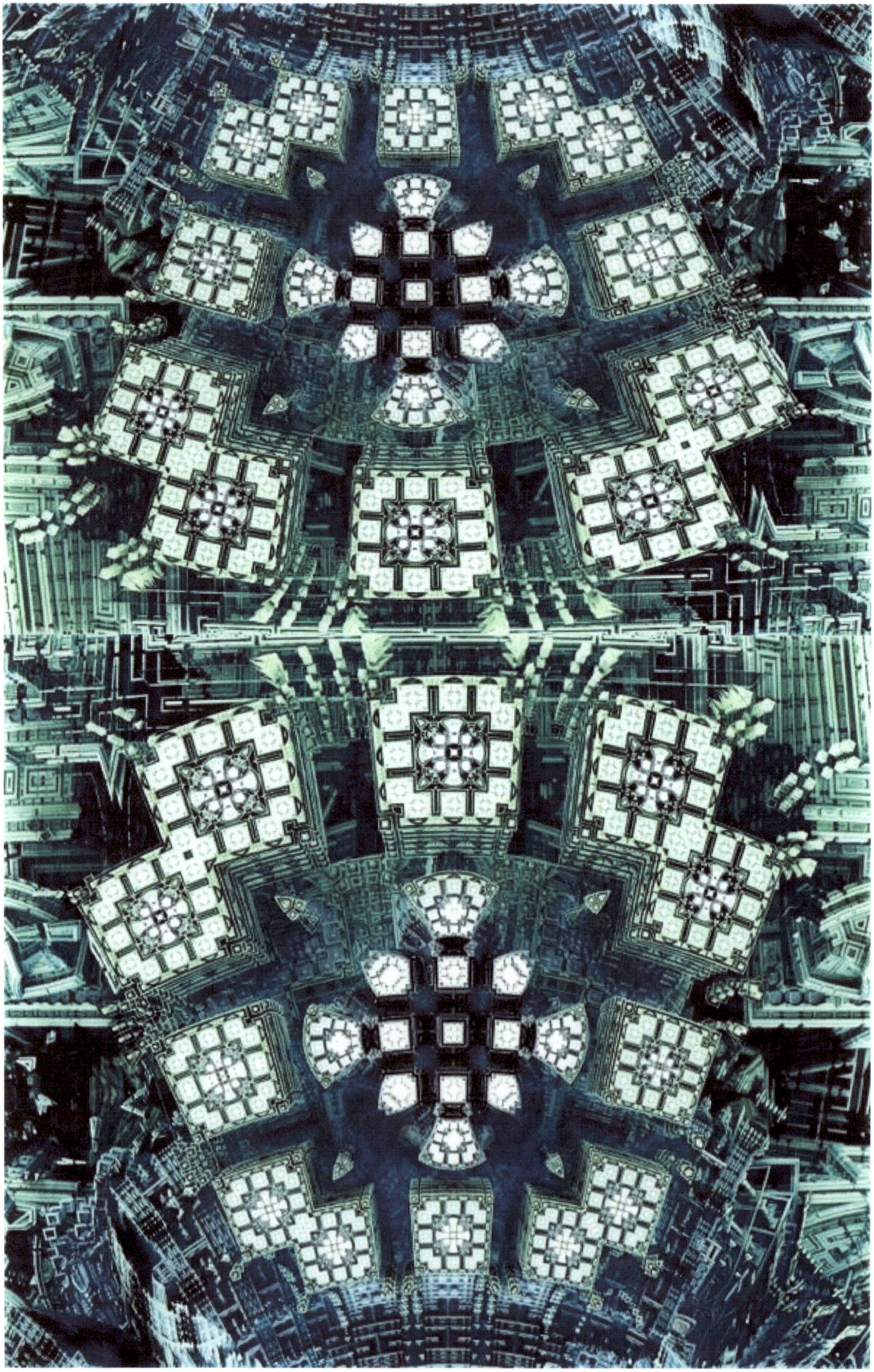

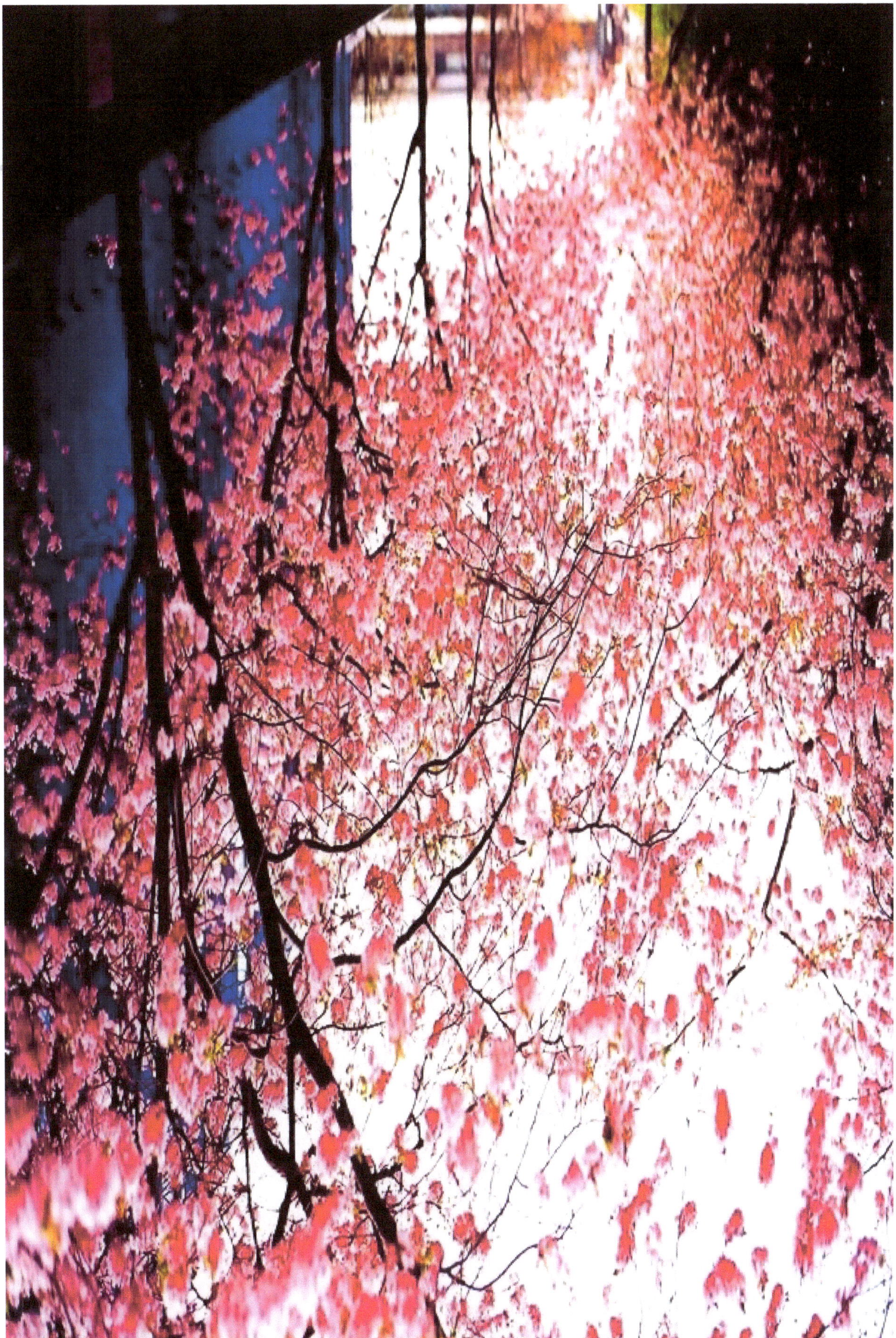

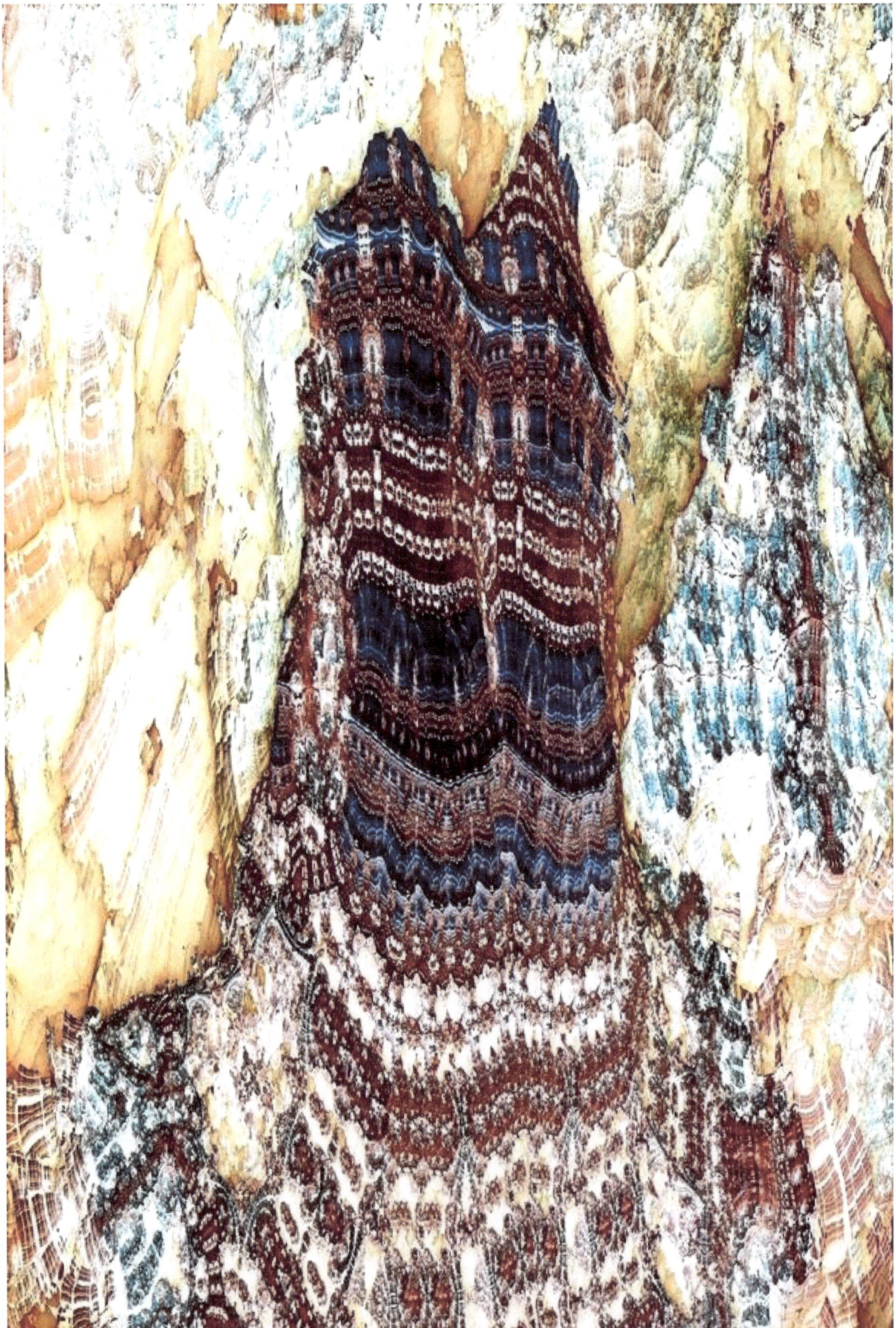

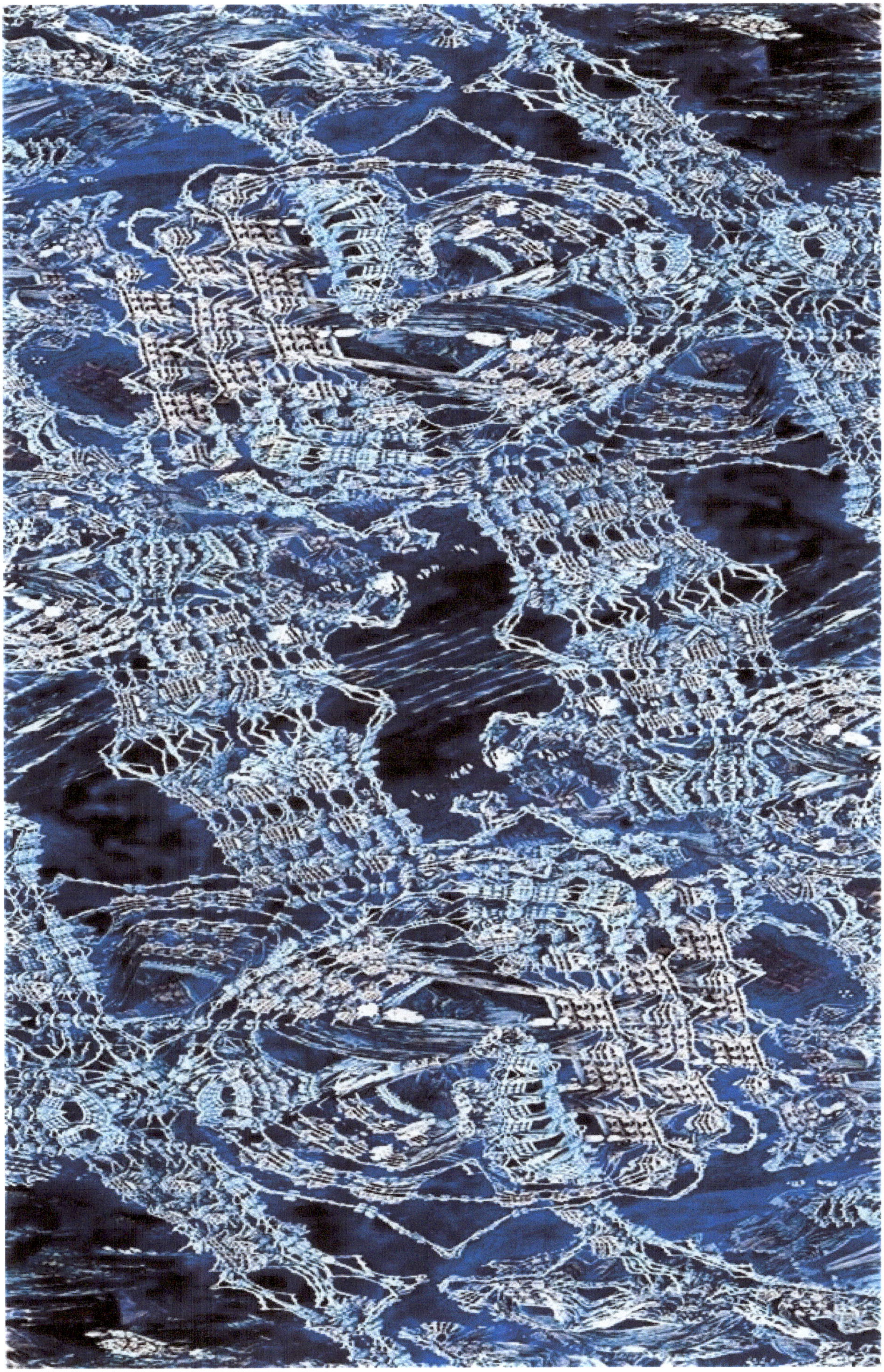

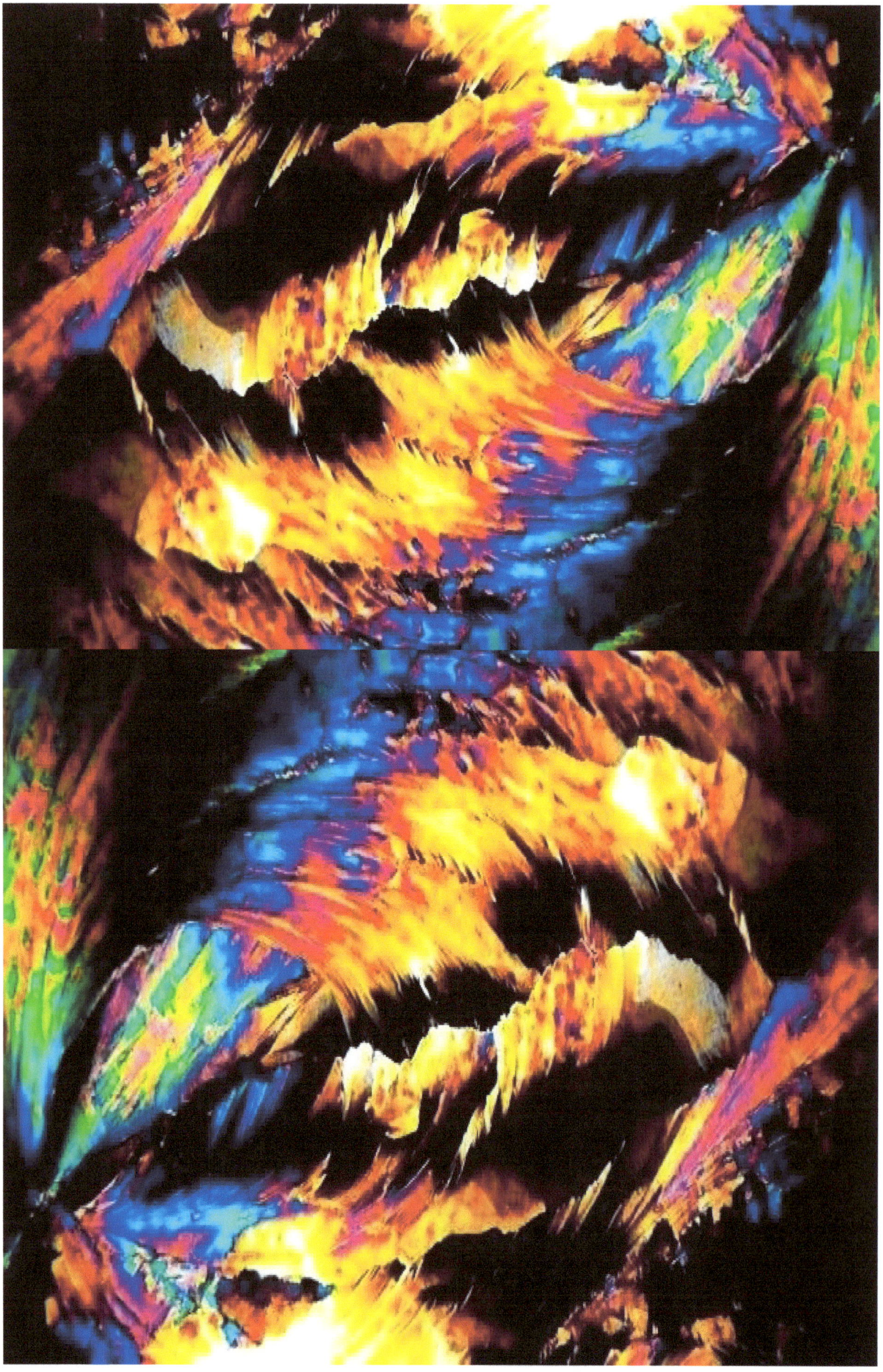

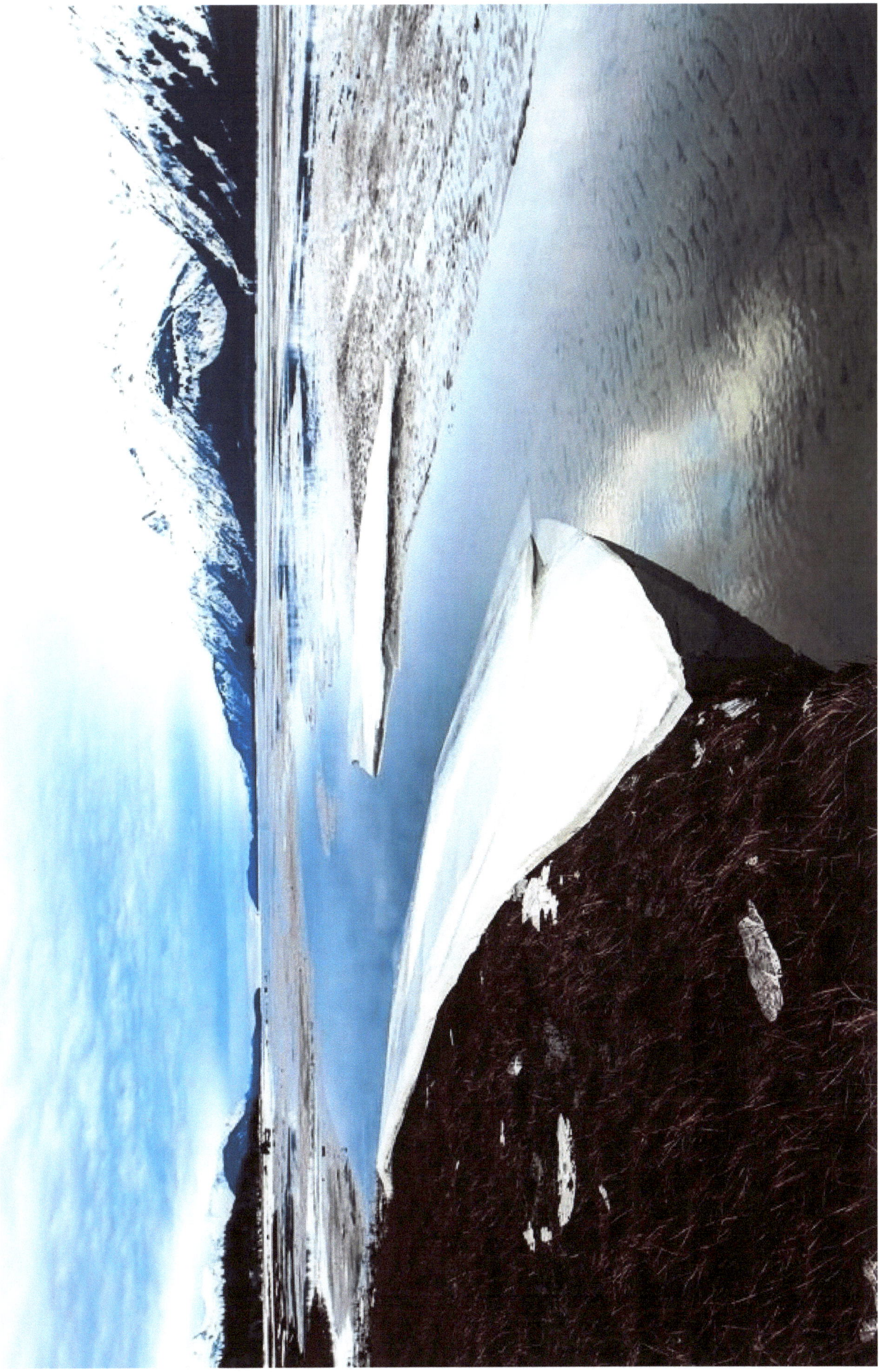

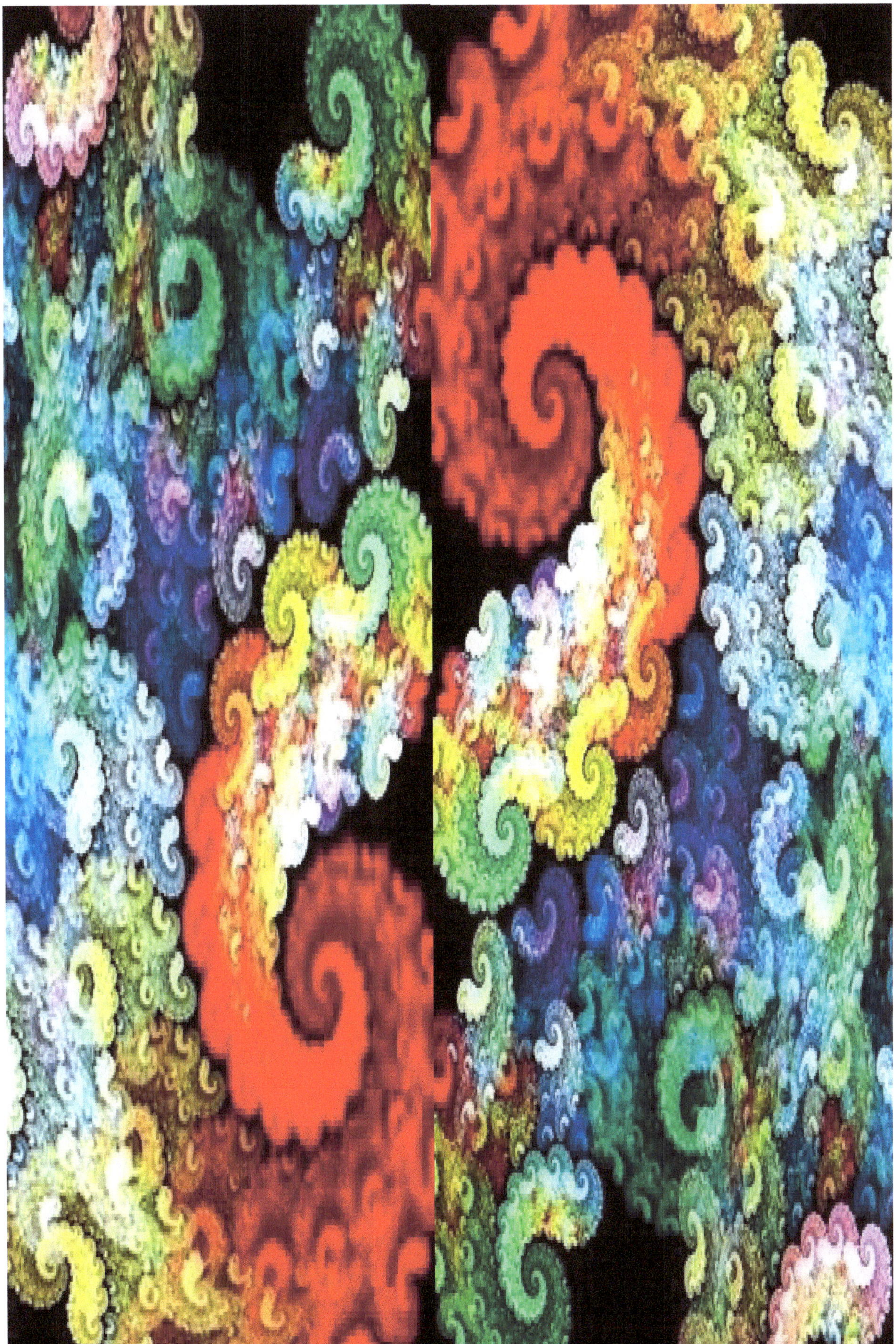

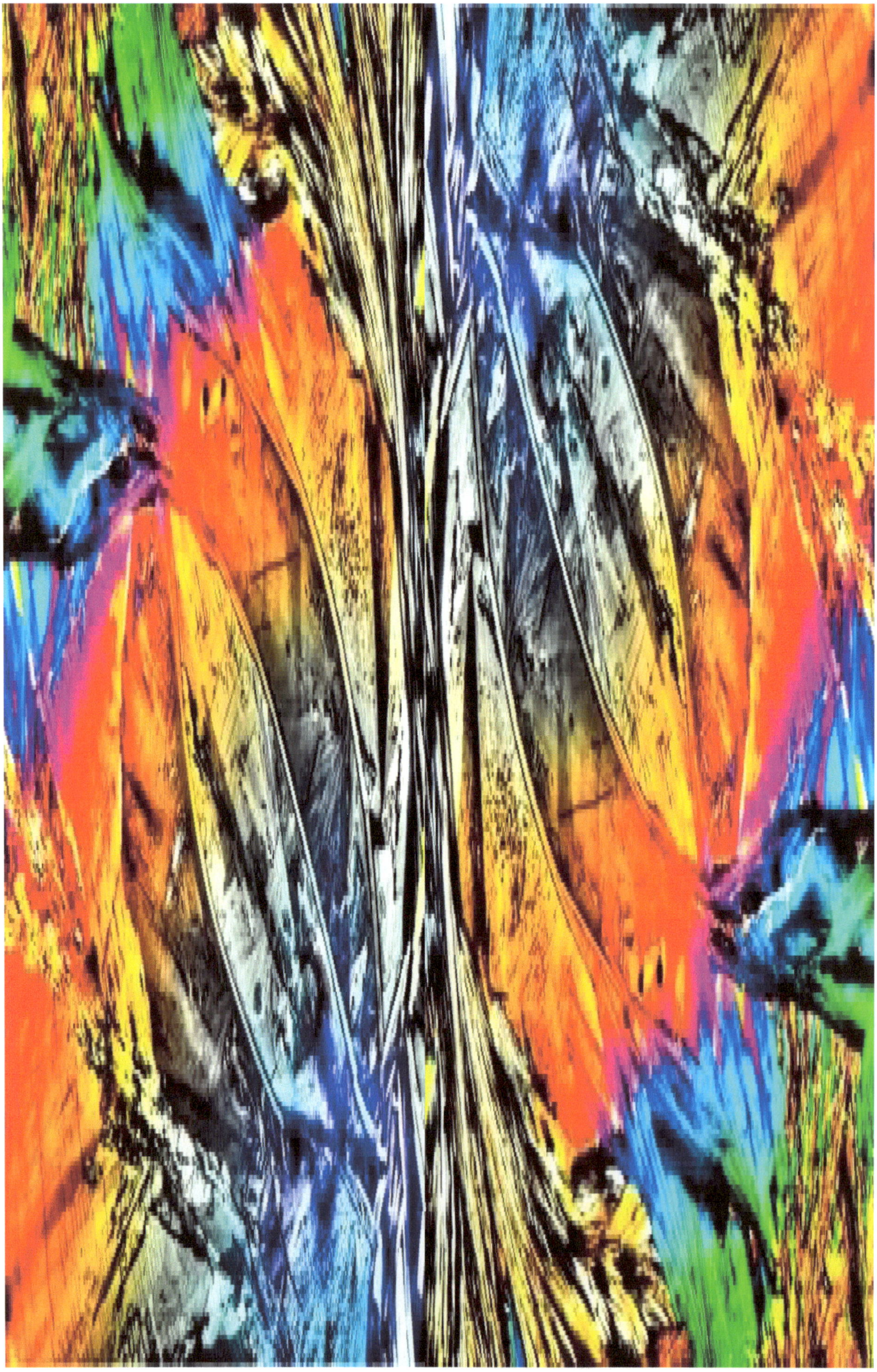

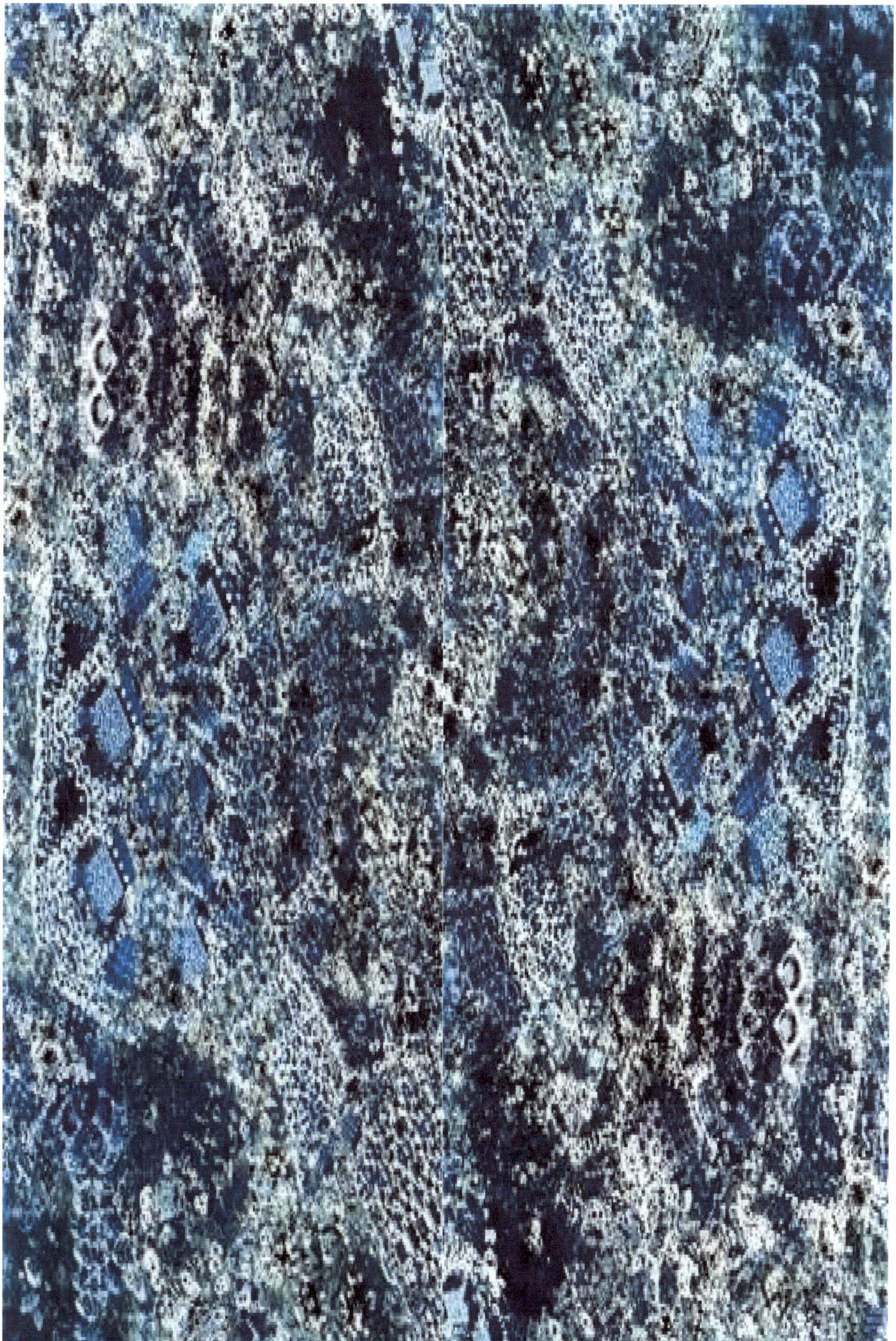

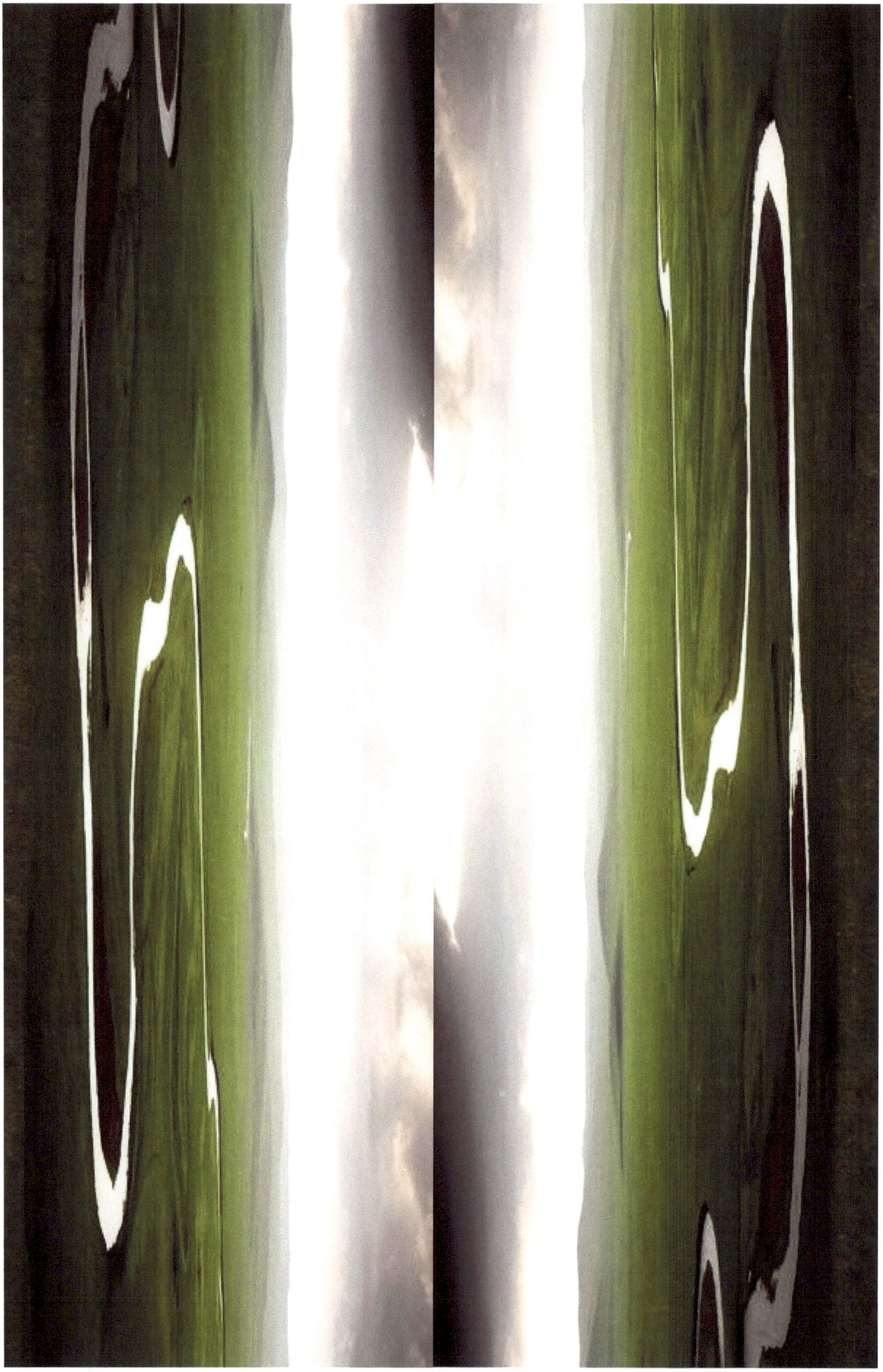

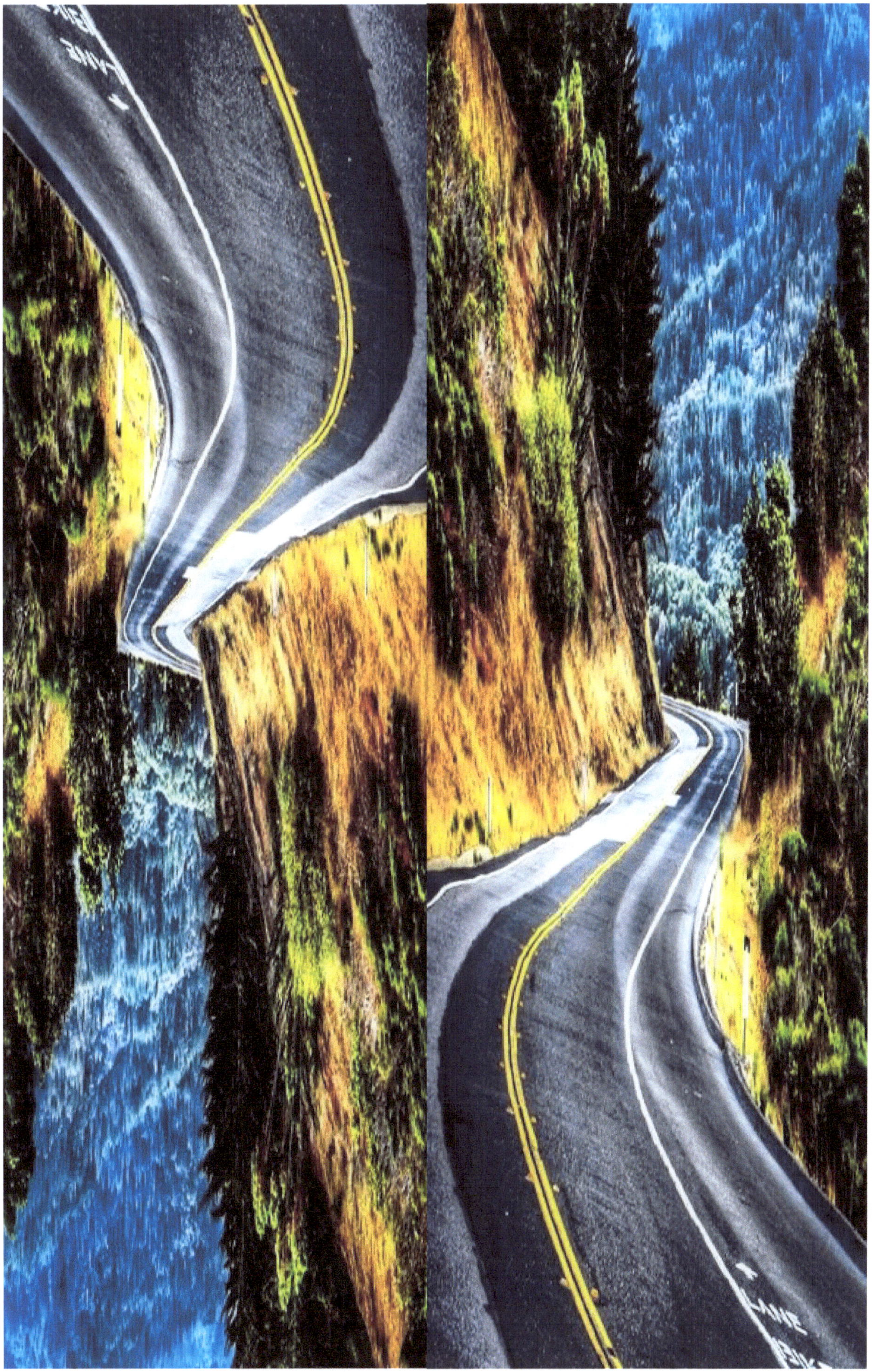

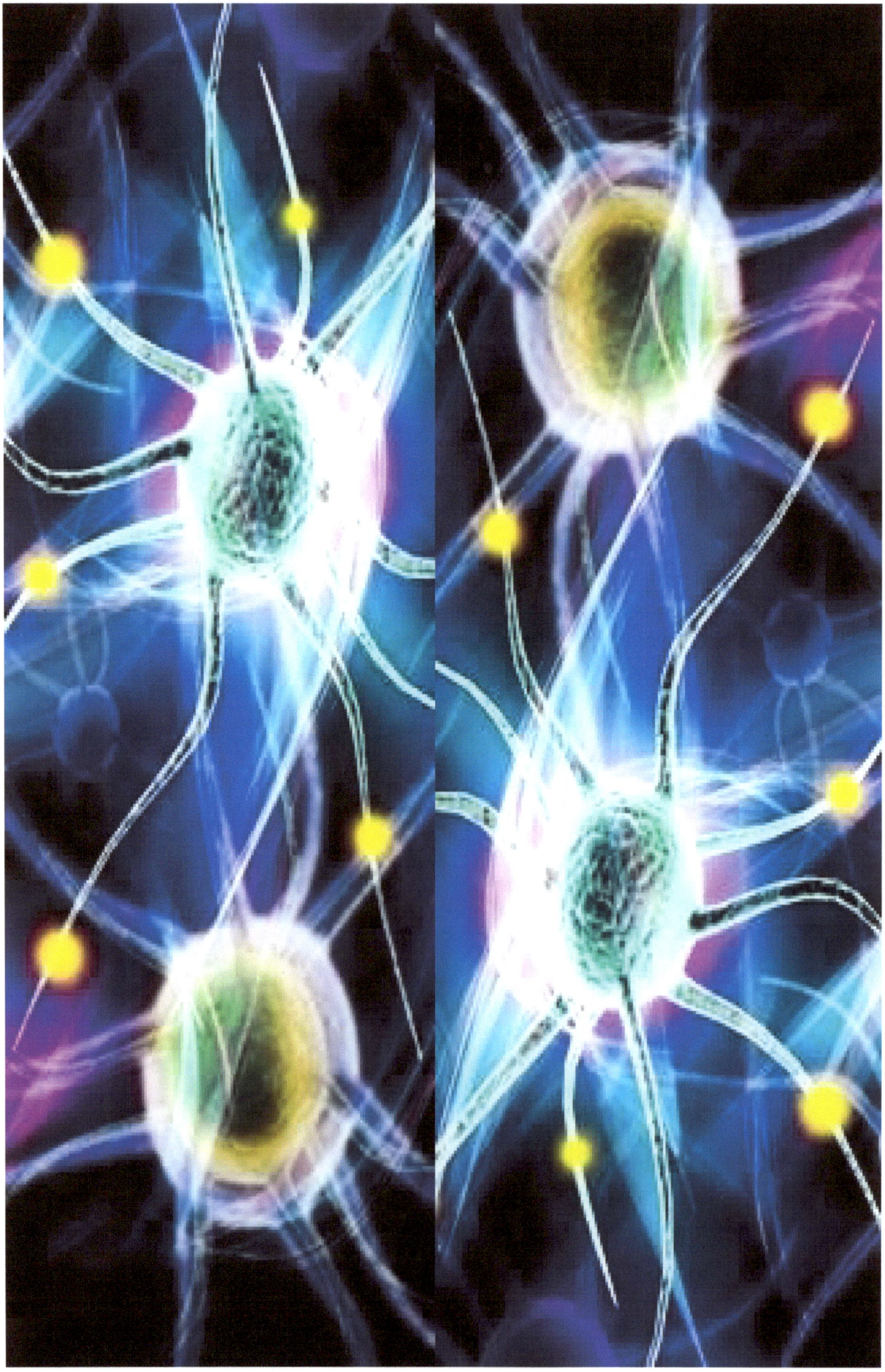

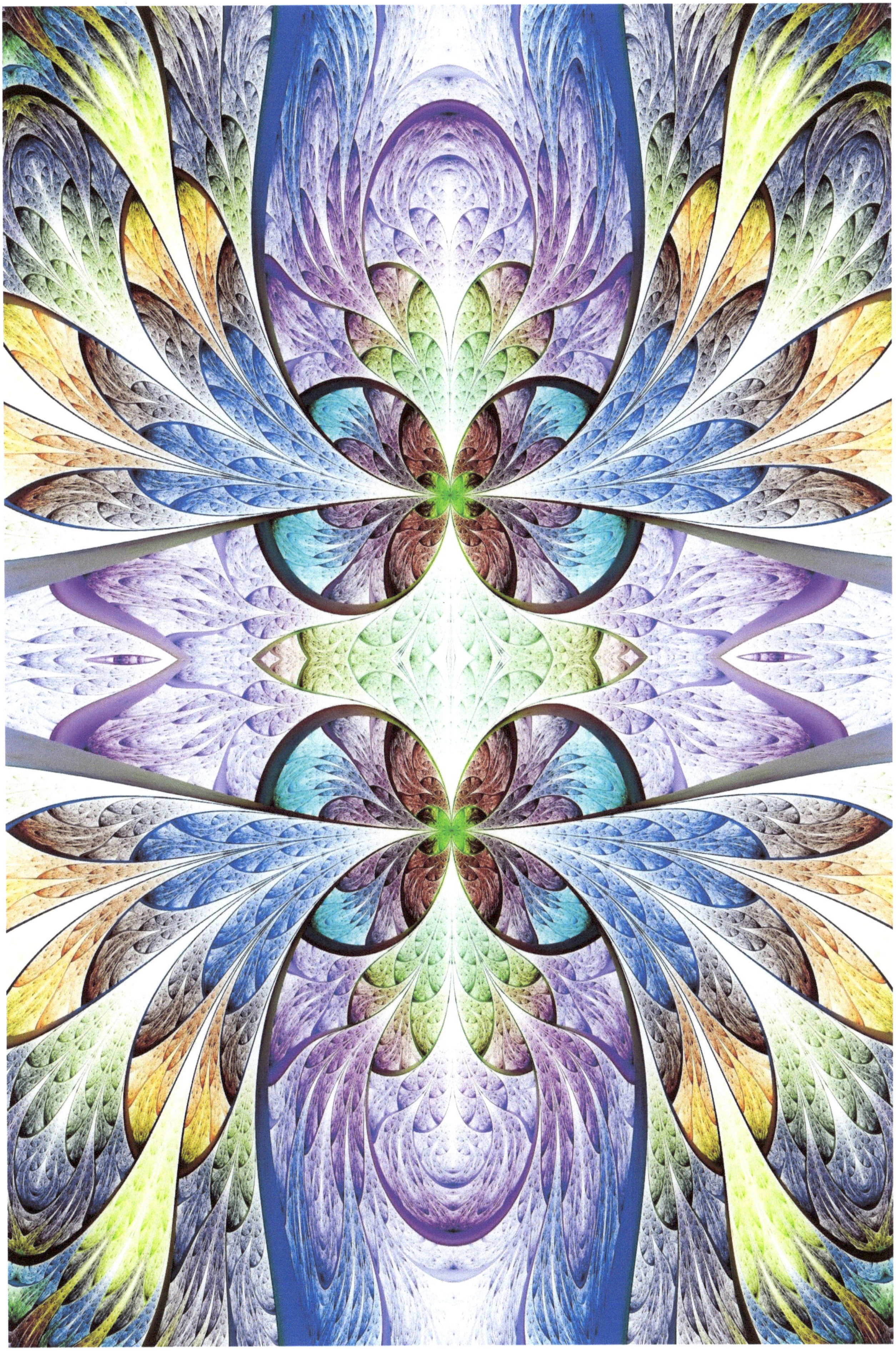

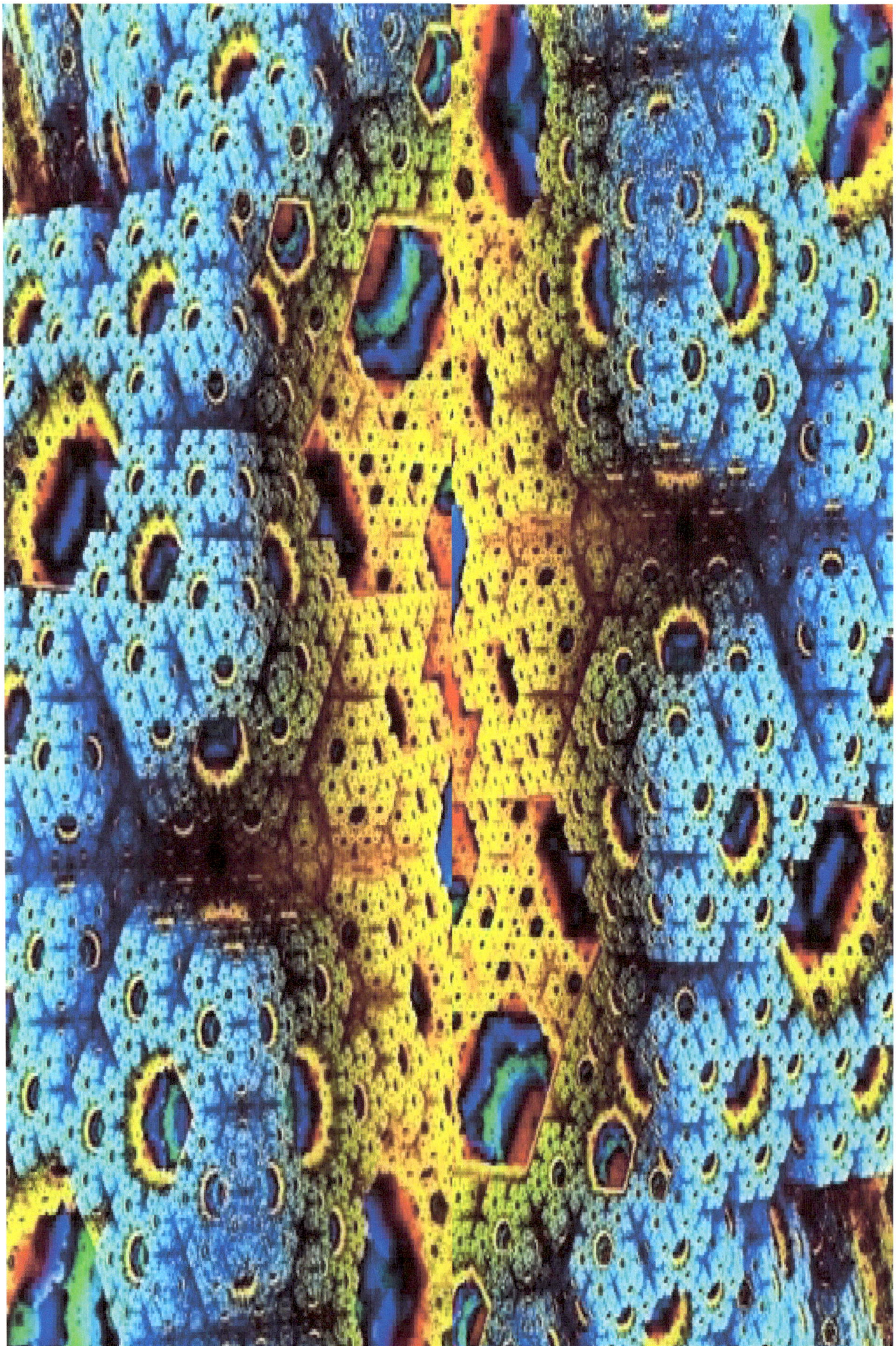

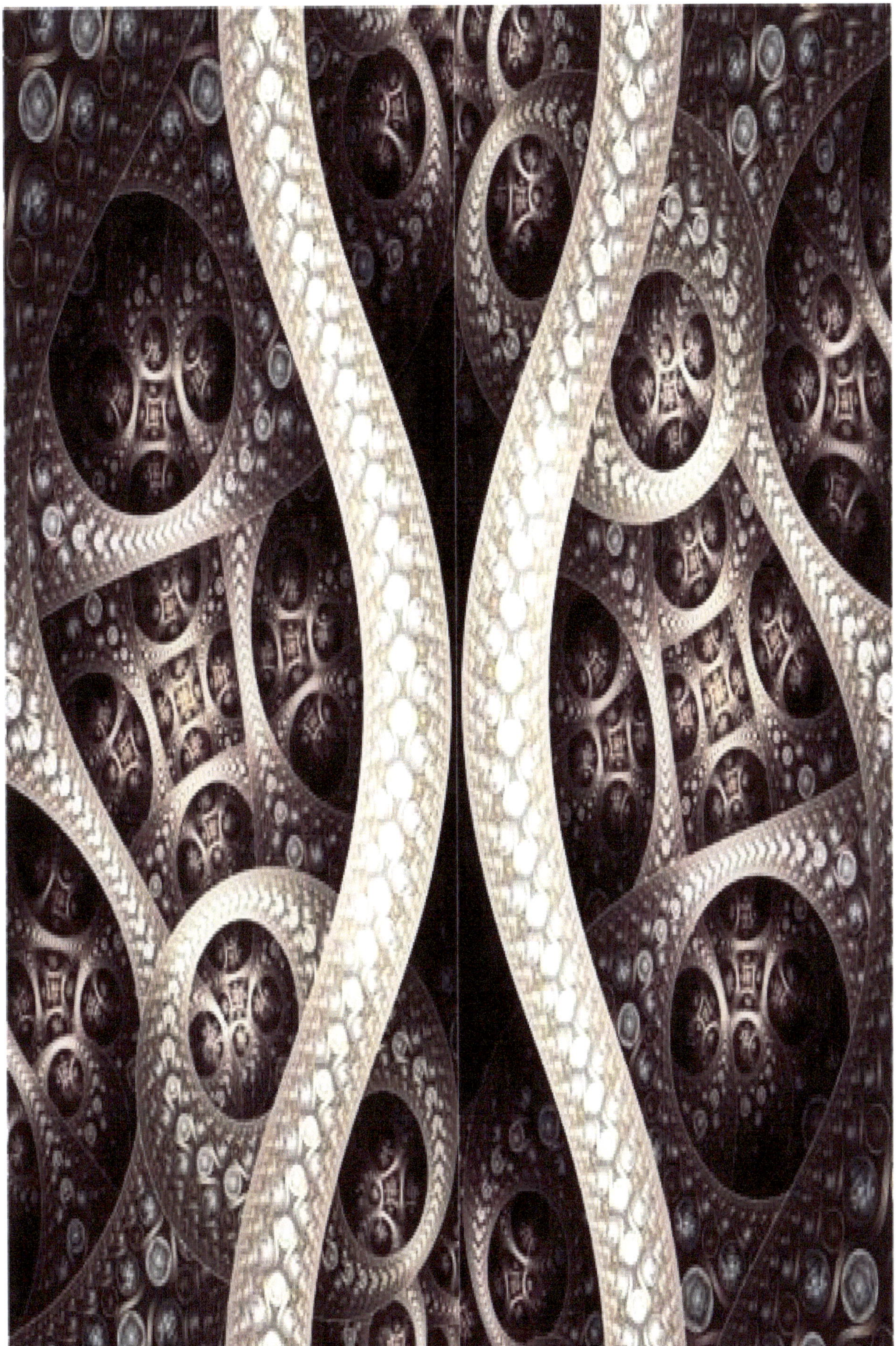

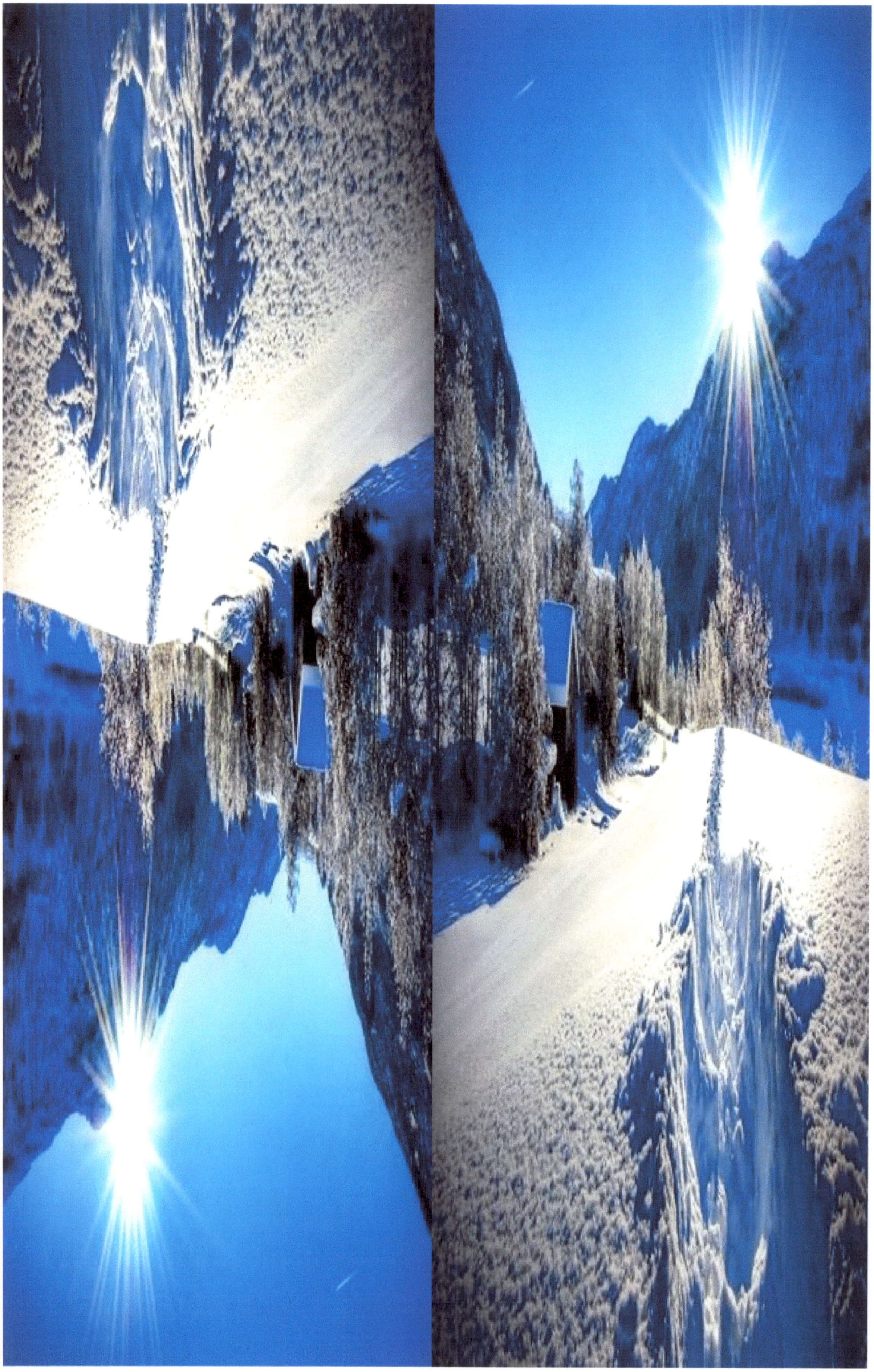

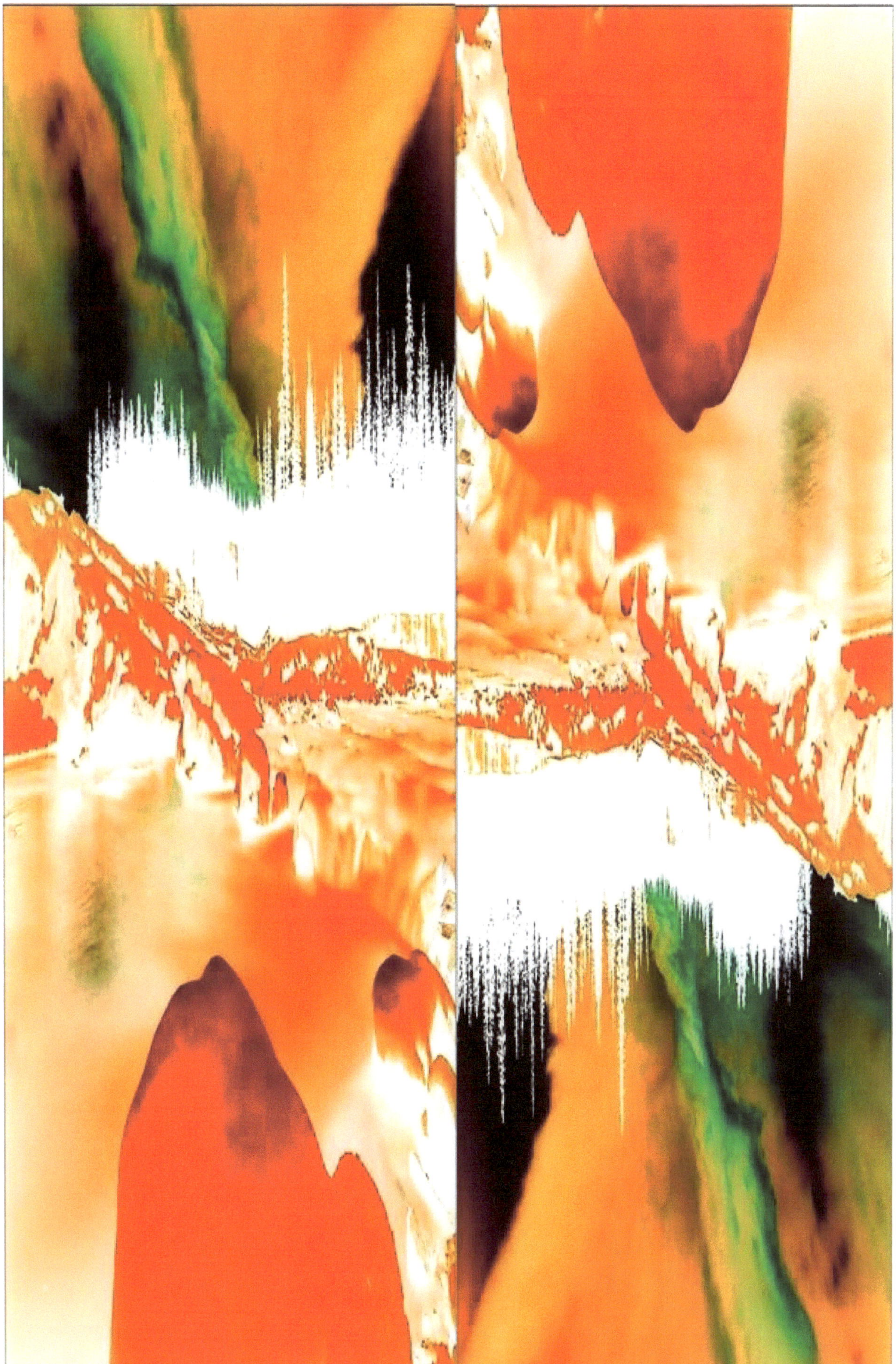

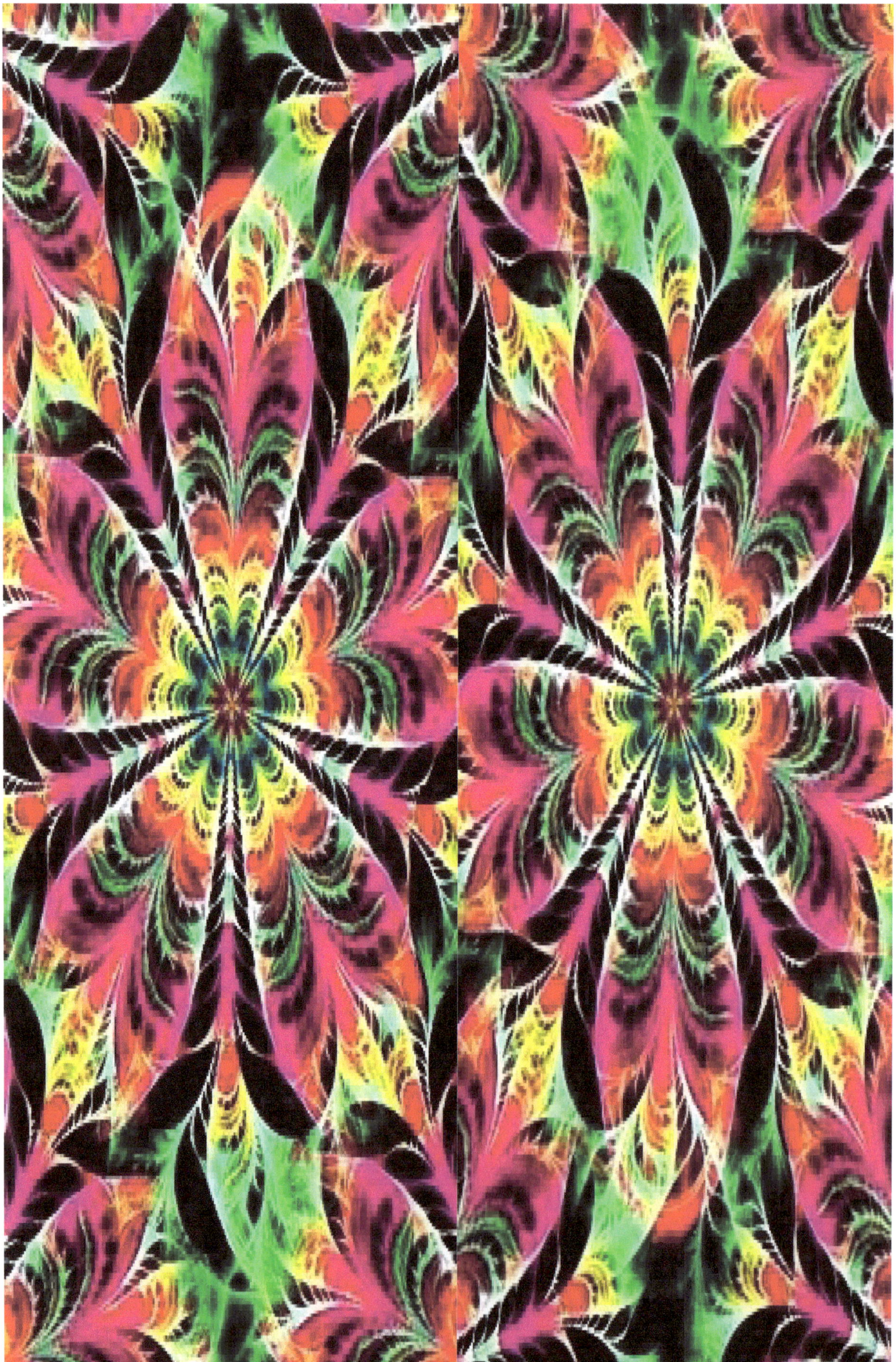

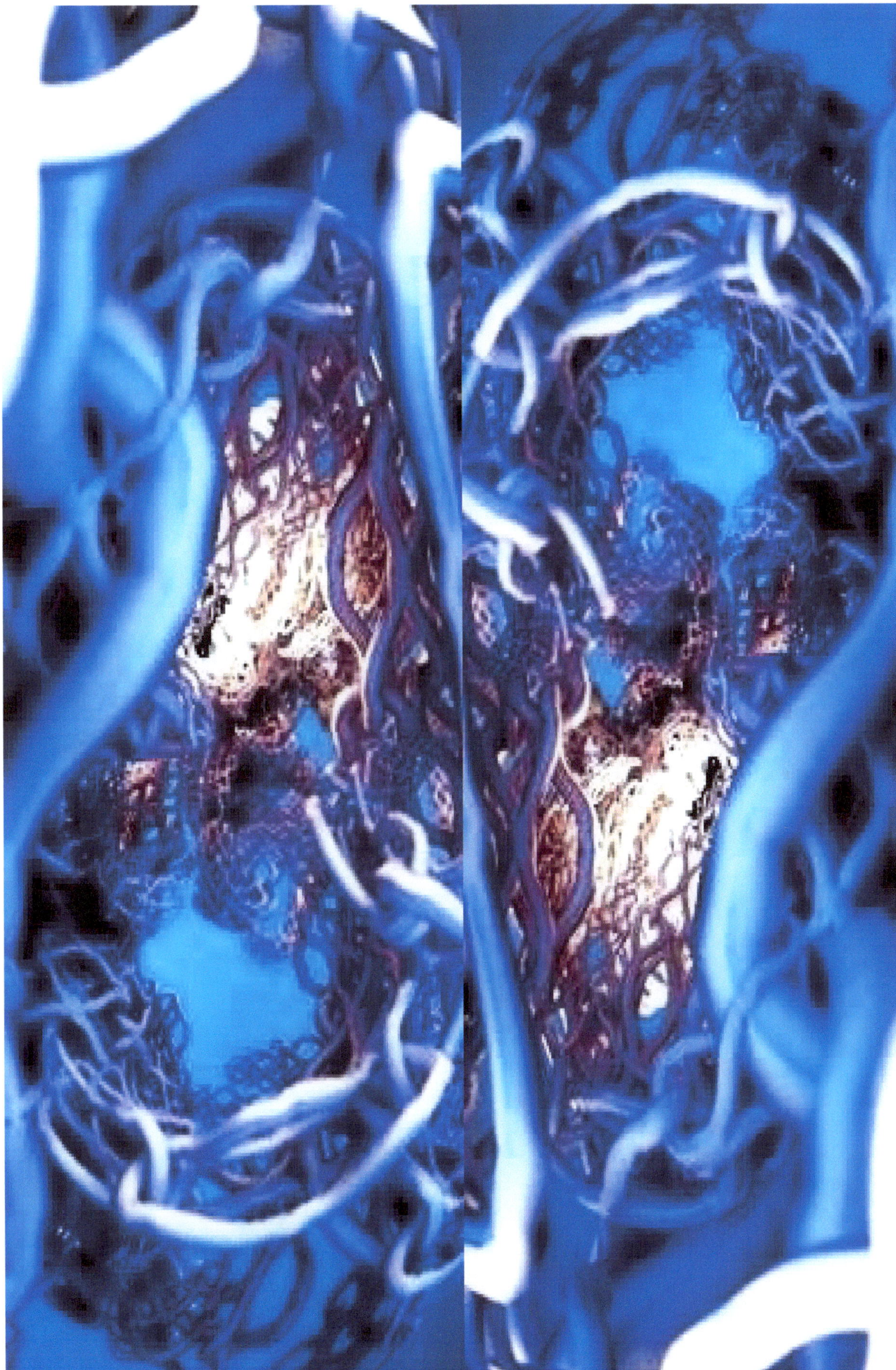

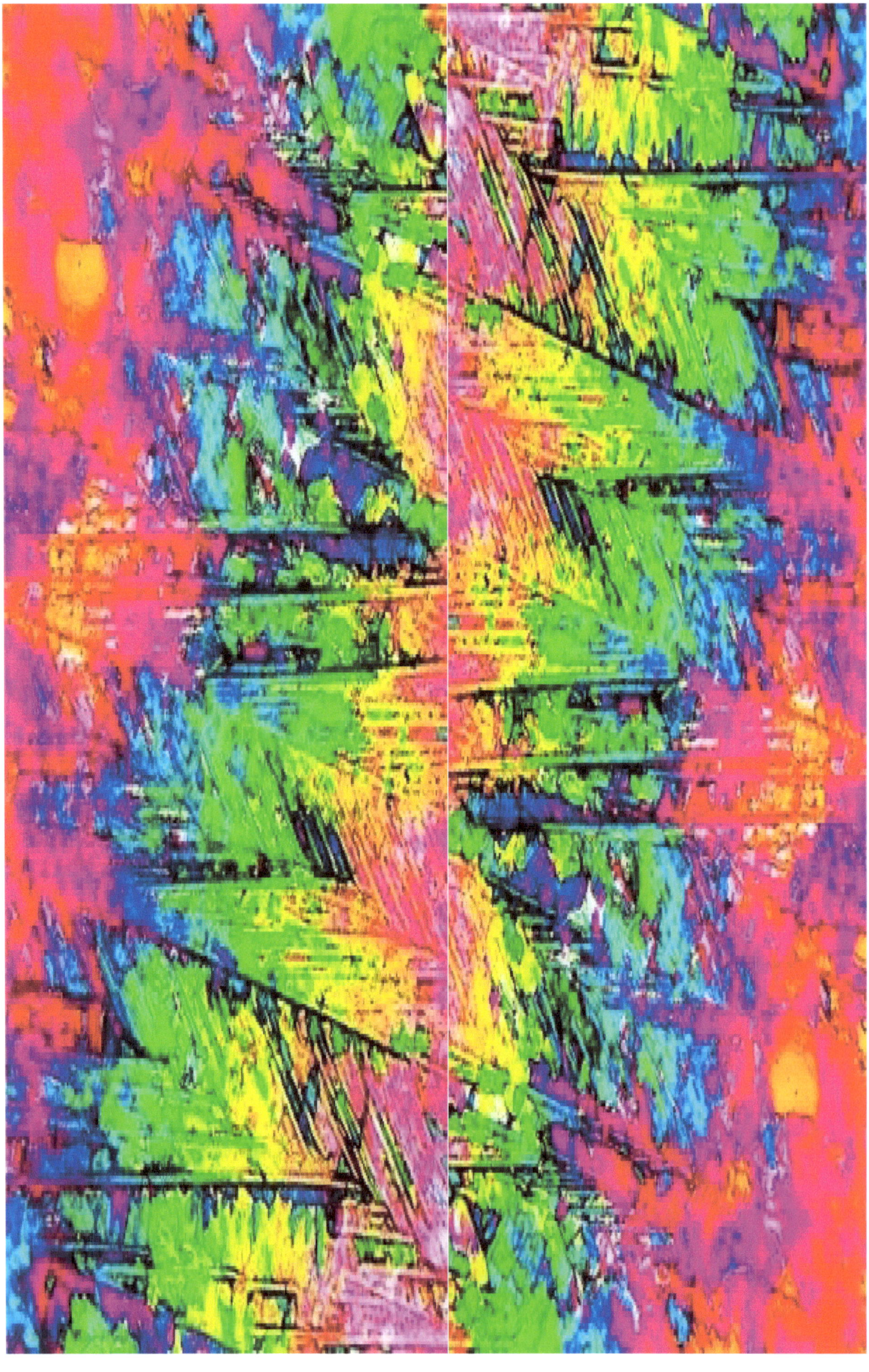

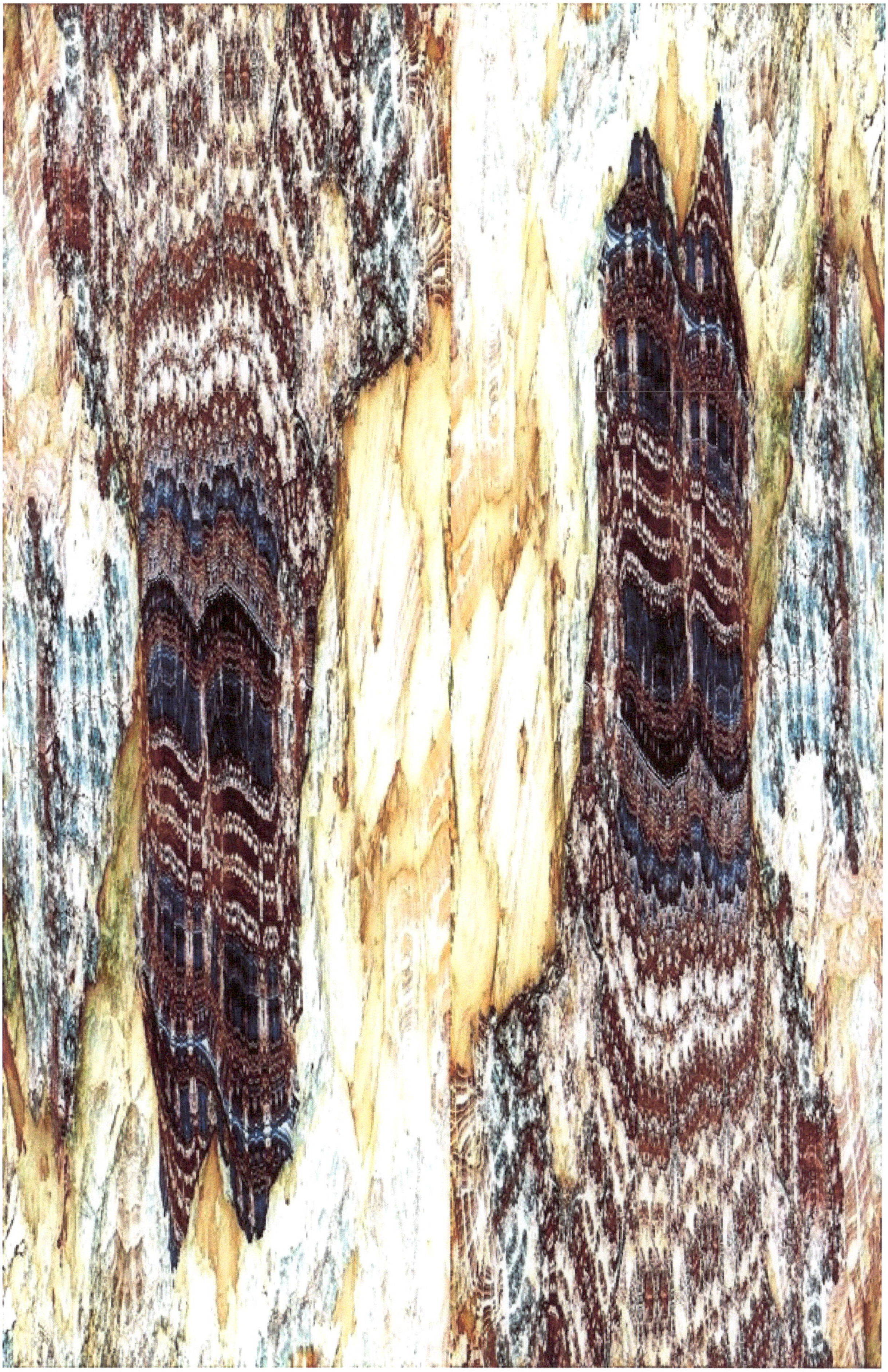

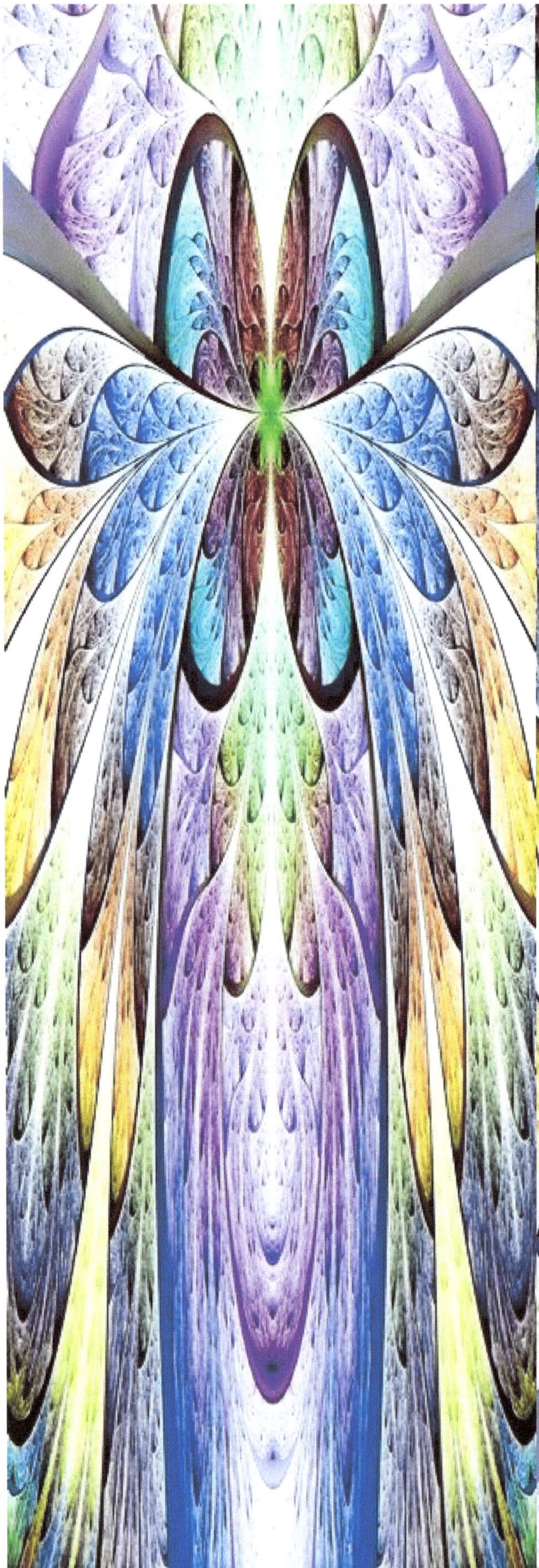
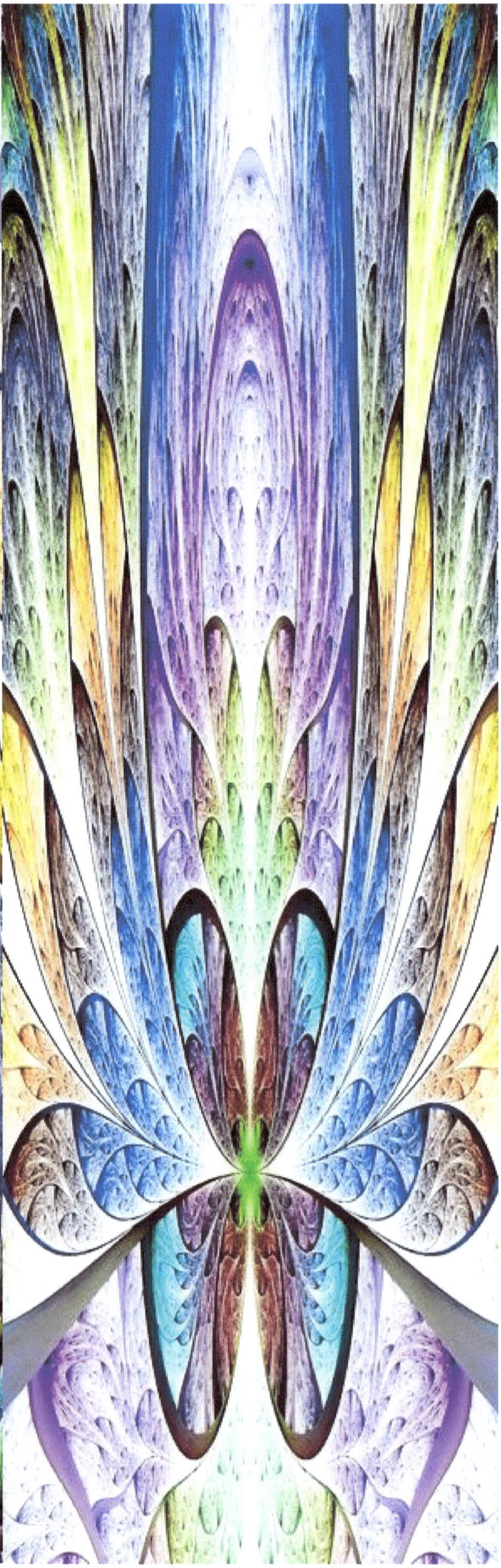

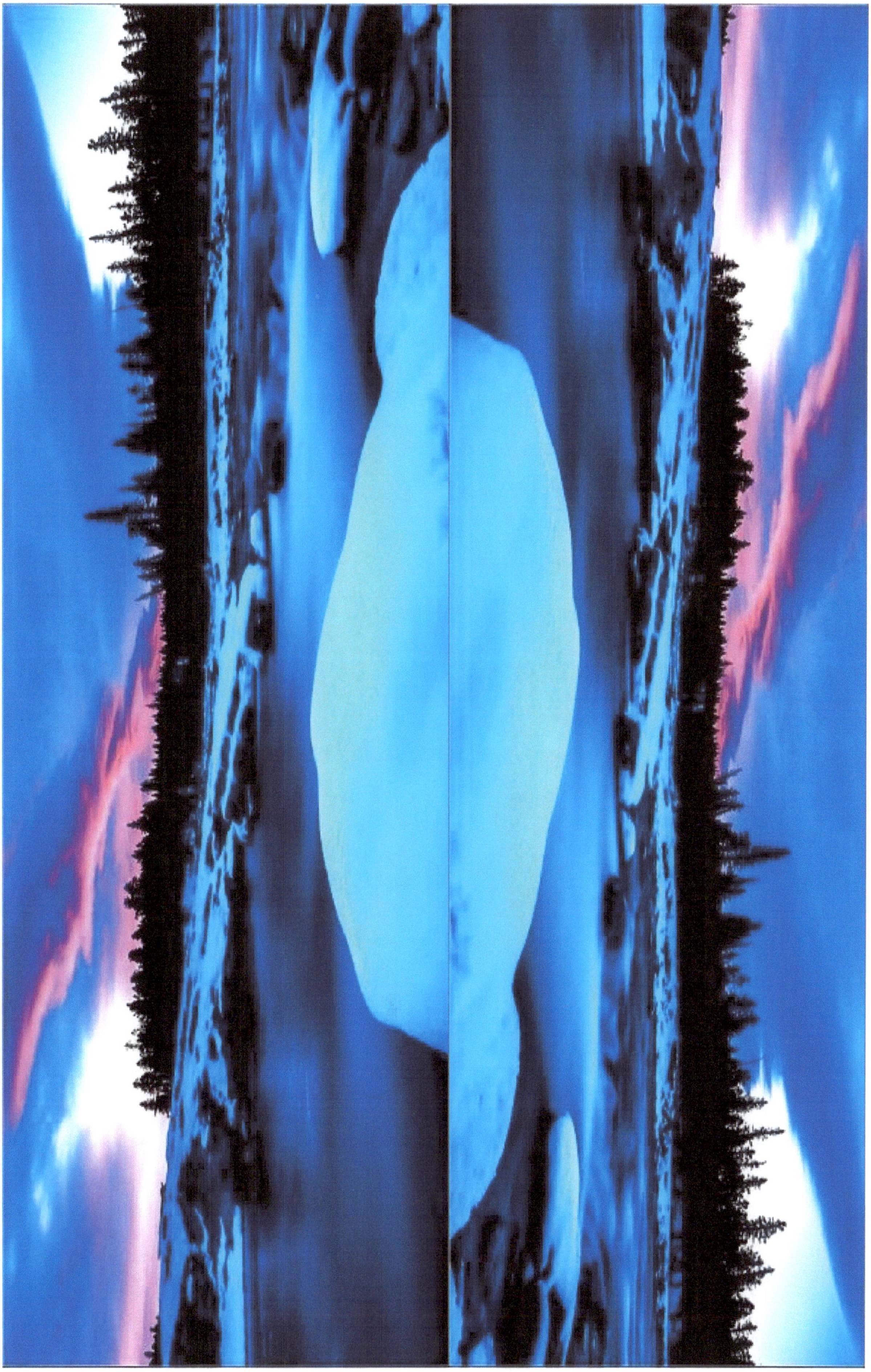

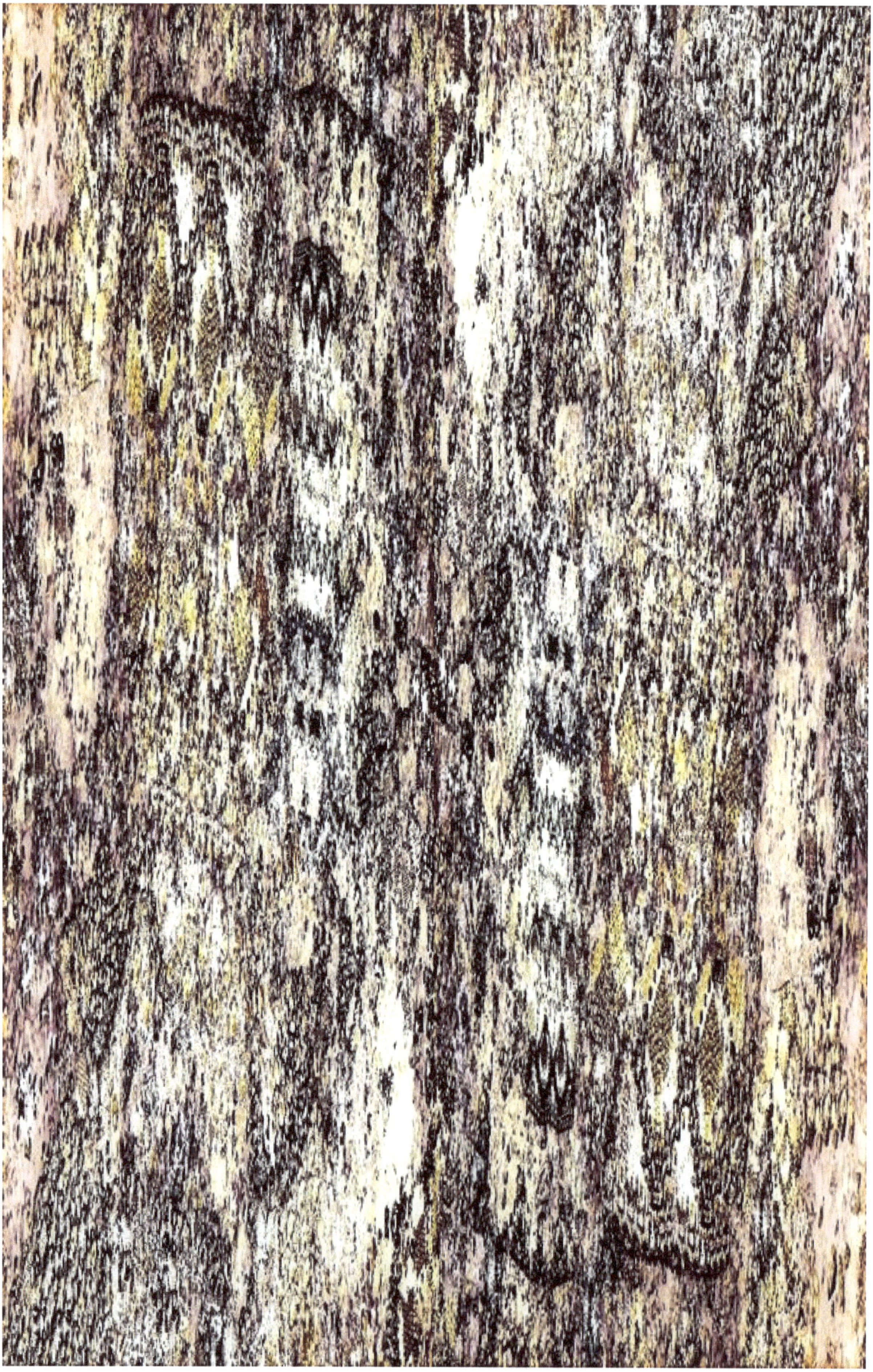

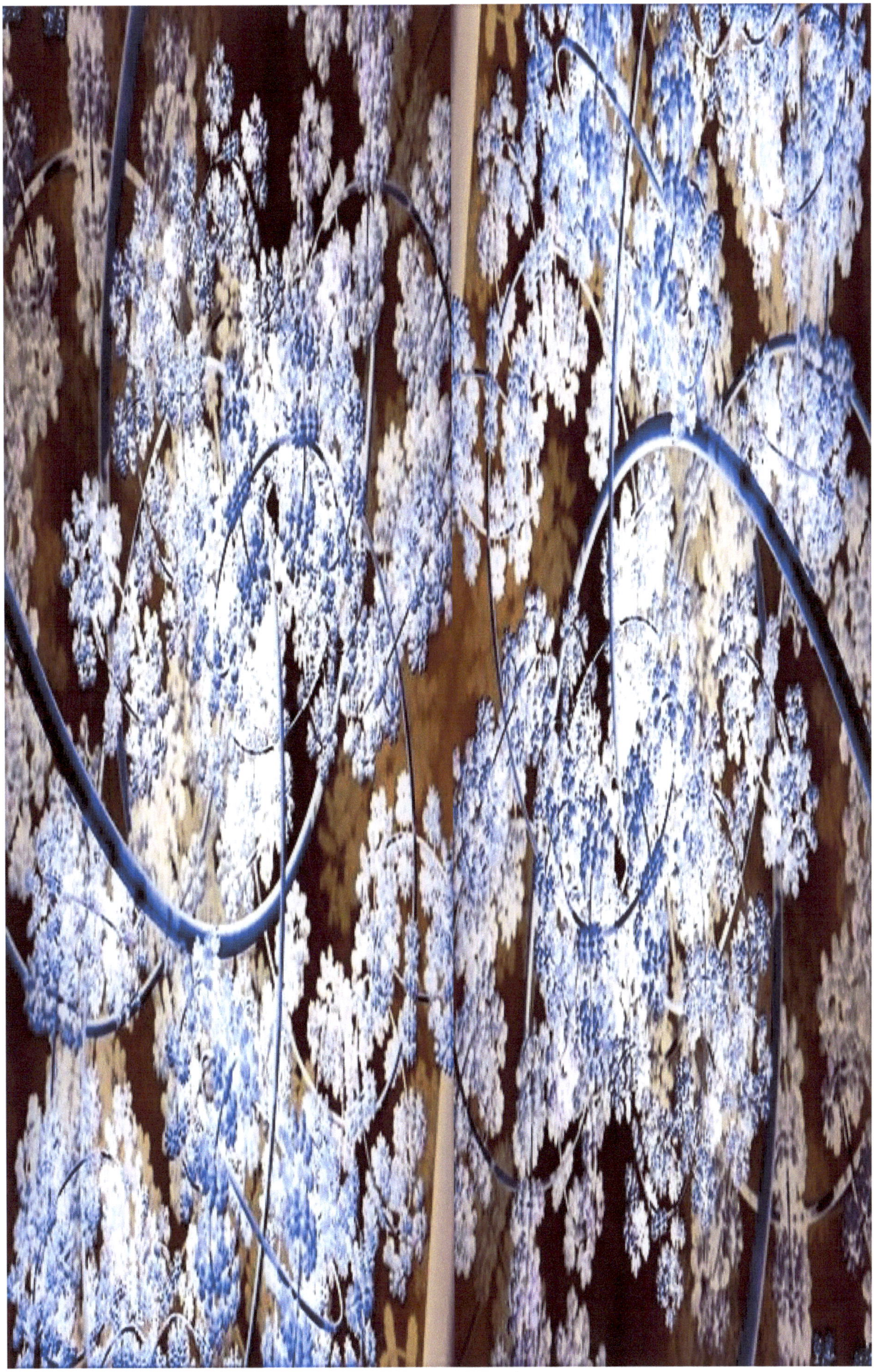

Imagination Arya Bàhram

www.ingramcontent.com/pod-product-compliance
Lightning Source LLC
Chambersburg PA
CBHW051221220526
45473CB00003B/1118
9781718715530